WITCHCRAFT IN EUROPE
AND THE NEW WORLD,
1400–1800

Related titles:

Languages of Witchcraft   *Edited by Stuart Clark*

The Occult in Early Modern Europe   *Edited by P.G. Maxwell-Stuart*

Witchcraft and Magic in Sixteenth- and Seventeenth-Century Europe, 2nd edition   *Geoffrey Scarre and John Callow*

Witchcraft in Europe and the New World, 1400–1800

P. G. Maxwell-Stuart

palgrave

First published 2001 by
PALGRAVE
Houndmills, Basingstoke, Hampshire RG21 6XS and
175 Fifth Avenue, New York, N. Y. 10010
Companies and representatives throughout the world

PALGRAVE is the new global academic imprint of
St. Martin's Press LLC Scholarly and Reference Division and
Palgrave Publishers Ltd (formerly Macmillan Press Ltd).

ISBN: 978-0-333-76465-7

This book is printed on paper suitable for recycling and made from fully managed and sustained forest sources.

A catalogue record for this book is available from the British Library.

Library of Congress Cataloging-in-Publication Data
Maxwell-Stuart, P. G.
     Witchcraft in Europe and the New World, 1400–1800 /
P.G. Maxwell-Stuart.
          p. cm.
     Includes bibliographical references and index.

          1. Witchcraft—Europe—History. 2. Witchcraft—America–
–History. I. Title.
     BF1584.E85 M39 2000
     133.4'3'09—dc21
                                                              00–066869

Transferred to Digital Printing 2012

Contents

List of Figures

The following are taken from Ulrich Molitor's *De Lamiis et Phitonicis Mulieribus*, published in 1489.

Preface

This book has been written for students and for the interested general reader. My own students have suggested to me that what they would find most helpful would be neither a collection of anecdotal material, nor a survey of Western European witchcraft so abbreviated as to be little better than a shopping-list of famous names and events, but a succinct guide to some of the principal themes of the subject with enough accompanying illustrative material to make the various points, and direct the reader to more extensive treatments. This I have tried to do in the following pages. All translations in the text are my own.

The bibliography of witchcraft is now vast, and in consequence the list of books and articles I have given here is intended only to provide initial reading matter stemming from what is discussed in this book. There is a great deal of interesting work being published in languages other than English. Unfortunately much of this remains unused. In reluctant recognition that monoglottism is the norm rather than the exception, I have included only a few works in French, German and Italian. But the reader should note that dependence on English-language works alone will deprive him or her of some of the best modern scholarship in this area.

P. G. M.-S.

1

Themes and Definitions

Preliminary Remarks

One of the great dangers for the student of witchcraft is to fall into the trap of conceiving it in terms of some kind of monolithic set of beliefs and practices unaltering throughout the diverse geography of Europe, and unchanged by time or circumstance. Nothing, as common sense suggests, could be further from the truth. Magic (of which witchcraft is merely a particular example) was believed in, of course, and practised from ancient to modern times both within and beyond those geographical bounds – not as an alternative religion, but as a customary and expected companion to the official faith. It was, in fact, the unavoidable concomitant of belief in supernatural and preternatural realms of existence, and it had its own multiplicity of individual tenets and practices, the existence of which presented anyone who might try to exercise control over them with an opponent more akin to a hydra than a giant.

This multiplicity necessarily posed a problem for the Church which had to decide whether she should come to terms with magic and, as it were, incorporate its views and ceremonies within her own; or tolerate them, while offering condemnation in as moderate a tone as decency and official self-regard would allow; or try to root them out, with all the attendant difficulties such an attempt would inevitably entail. What the Church actually did at any given time depended, of course, on many considerations, not all of them spiritual, and one can detect quiescent and persecutory phases in official attitudes, both ecclesiastical and secular, towards magicians (many of whom were members of the clergy) and witches throughout the whole of the Mediaeval period.

It would be unhistorical to suggest that the Church was sceptical over the fact of magic, the existence of spirits good and bad, and the ability of both spirits and magicians, male or female, to manipulate the forces of nature in such a way as to produce effects which, to those who did not understand how they managed such things, might appear to be miraculous or, at the very least, extraordinary. The Church's reservations were based, rather, on the notion that no spirit, good or evil, could accomplish more than was allowed by the laws of creation, which had been laid down by the Creator himself, and that in consequence their power was limited, even though to humans, whose knowledge of those same laws was so much less than that of the spirits, it might seem limitless. Nor could spirits do anything without God's permission, and this represented another, formidable boundary to their power. So the Church's scepticism referred to what one might call the logistics of Satan's battle with humanity. Was any given type, or even act, of malefice really possible within the constraints God had placed on diabolical power? Considerations such as these underlie St Thomas Aquinas's discussions of magic and demonology and were to last throughout later periods of debate between theologians, lawyers and physicians when prosecution of witches became a dominant manifestation of particular strains attendant upon European intellectual discussion of the nature of God and creation.

Literary Models

Later ideas about magic and witchcraft were not unique to Christians, of course. Practitioners of magic in Mediaeval Europe inherited from the Greeks and Romans a long tradition of both amateur and professional attempts to manipulate the natural and supernatural worlds with a view to achieving, for their own gratification, ends such as curing illness, divining the future or destroying one's enemies, which it was believed would not have been attainable by any other means. These same practitioners also inherited an expectation that authority, whether secular or religious, despite long periods of apparent toleration, was likely to disapprove and be suspicious of their activities and so intermittently take steps (sometimes ineffectual but sometimes brutally effective) to curb or put a stop to their practices.

In addition to this two-fold Classical inheritance, of course, there existed the magical customs of numberless communities scattered the length and breadth of the Roman Empire, each with its own tradition of practice both verbal and ritual, and yet open to change and influence as war, famine, disease or missionary religion swept strangers through their midst or removed individuals and groups from one place to another. Conceptions of and notions relating to operators of magic therefore reflected this Classical inheritance and local diversity, embodying themselves in the imaginations of succeeding generations and there fostering preconceptions which later Mediaeval and early modern scholars strove, with varying degrees of success, to align with the popular beliefs they knew and experienced.

Greek and Latin literature contain several vivid portraits of female magicians. Homer provides Circe, and Euripides Medea, both beautiful, but also dangerous and malevolent women, and this image was one which several artists such as Dürer, Baldung Grien, and (perhaps) Van Eyck used to great effect, especially when it was contrasted with that of an old, ugly witch, as in one of the pictures by Hans Franck. Nevertheless, the youthful, beautiful witch was not the image which best suited polemic, and when anti-magical polemic became increasingly important at the end of the fifteenth century, it concentrated upon another part of the Classical tradition – the witch as crone or hag. From this, artistic and literary expectation preferred to draw a picture of ugliness and stupidity such as that which we can see in a set of drawings by Hieronymus Bosch, or of malice and lust for illegitimate power, such as the description of Erictho by the Roman poet Lucan, one of the most popular Latin writers in the Mediaeval educational canon.

> The face of the sacrilegious woman is in the grip of a repulsive, wasting thinness. It never sees the bright, cheerful sky and is tainted by the yellowish pallor of the necromancer. A mass of matted hair is piled on top of it.... If there is a sudden burst of rain and pitch-black clouds sweep away the stars. it is then that the witch ventures out from graves which have been stripped of their contents, and tries, under cover of darkness, to grasp hold of the lightning-flashes. She tramples and stamps upon the seeds of fertile corn and causes them to shrivel, and any air which does not bring death she corrupts by breathing upon it.
> (See further **52**, 190–8)

Here we have many of the ingredients which were to go into the construction of the witch's later stereotype. She is female, ugly, malicious, and either mad or deluded. She has no reverence for established religion. She does her work at night. It is implied that she makes use of corpses in her magic. She is connected with death, violent storms and the destruction of crops, and she actively taints the air which thereby turns into a cause of fatal diseases.

Lucan calls her 'Thessala' in reference to the women of Thessaly who were renowned for their magical abilities; but Latin furnished other, more common terms for 'witch' which both mirrored a variety of popular beliefs and, by constant repetition both in the written word and in learned conversation, helped to spread and reinforce those beliefs among the educated classes throughout Western Europe. Thus, *strix* referred to a kind of owl regarded as a bird of ill omen and so emphasised the conception of the witch as someone whose appearance would bode no good, who could change her shape, fly through the air, and who operated mainly during the night. *Lamia* was originally the name of a female monster who was said to eat children, and so when employed to mean 'witch', the word conveyed the ideas of ugliness, infanticide and cannibalism [64]. *Sortilega*, on the other hand, designated someone who foretold the future by throwing lots and reading their messages, and similarly *saga*, etymologically connected with words which refer to foreboding, presentiment and the ability to predict or sniff out the future, came to refer to a person who attempted to mould the future and make it yield results which accorded with her will and intention.

We can see this last in a passage from the *Amores* of Ovid, another Roman poet widely read in Mediaeval schools. This tells us more of what witches were believed to do and how they did it.

Surely it is not an incantation and herbs which are doing me harm, poor wretch that I am? Surely a witch [*saga*] has not embedded my full name in an image made from blood-red wax and driven fine pins into the middle of its liver?

Ovid is complaining that something has rendered him impotent and that he suspects the cause is magical, and removing a man's sexual ability was one of the many charges which might be brought against Mediaeval and later witches, while the operation described by Ovid appears frequently in witchcraft literature.

Mediaeval guides for confessors, the *libri poenitentiales*, indicate that these Classical templates were used long after the pagan world

had supposedly vanished. The eleventh-century corrector of Burch-
ard of Worms, for example, prescribes penance on bread and water
for periods varying from ten days to two years for those who
consult magicians and seek to divine the future by casting lots;
who practise enchantment of objects with the intention of protecting
their animals from sickness while inflicting disease upon those of
another; who weave spells into their cloth or collect medicinal herbs
and chant non-Christian formulae over them; who raise storms or
change people's minds from love to hatred or from hatred into love.
Earlier eighth-century texts also inform us that a witch could be
called a 'vampire' and that some people believed witches, whether
male or female, ate human flesh [84].

Learned Categories of Magic

Ancient, Mediaeval and early modern writers on magic tend to
divide it into two types: not so much 'good' and 'bad' as 'bad'
and 'worse'. The former they call *mageia* and the latter *goeteia*.
Mageia was originally connected with the ancient Persian religion,
of which the *magos* was a priest. Hence *mageia* referred to rituals and
divinatory techniques conducted and practised by such priests. But
when the word passed into Greek, it took on a set of hostile mean-
ings (an example of one society's religious practices turning into
another's superstitions or demon-worship), and this inimical reinterpretation clung to it ever after. *Goeteia* comes from a Greek verb
meaning 'to wail or howl', and refers to the way in which magicians
were sad to give voice to magical incantations. Both words also
came to be associated with deceit and intellectual dishonesty. 'The
two techniques of *goeteia* and *mageia* are inventions', said the orator
Gorgias, 'and both of them produce spiritual aberrations and
fraudulent expectations.' No later Christian writer would have disagreed.

Deceit and intellectual dishonesty, however, can work in more
than one way. The magician may set out to deceive other people by
the use of techniques he or she knows do not work, or which appear
to work only because of the operator's skill in prestidigitation and
the arts of illusion – a type of magic the Mediaeval and early
modern world recognised and called *praestigia* (trickery) – or the
magician himself is deceived by the higher power or intelligence to
whom he directs his invocations, supplications and commands.

St Thomas Aquinas issued a warning against this possibility, adding that the intelligent being, who was the actual source from which the magician's arts derived their efficacy, was not one well-disposed towards virtue. Who, then, was deceiving whom? Could one be sure that the practice of magic was harmless or even beneficial when the likelihood was that the assisting power behind its effects was demonic rather than angelic? Moreover, if an evil spirit responded to a magician's invocation, did he do so because he was compelled by the magician's art, or because he chose to appear and help in order the more easily to ensnare the magician's soul and that of the magician's client? Here, in broad outline, was a theological debate which continued to be argued by writers on demonology throughout much of the early modern period and whose negative points were conveniently summed up by John Bromyard's *Handbook for Preachers* in 1348: magical practitioners are liars because they cannot accomplish what they promise; they are disobedient to divine, canon and civil law, all of which condemn and forbid their practices; and they are guilty of superstition and idolatry.

But does magic consist of a set of techniques which can be taught and learned, or does it stem from a natural ability, an inborn propensity inherited from one's parents? Some modern anthropologists, especially those writing about Africa, have drawn a distinction between the sorcerer who performs acts of harmful magic against other people, and the witch whose witchcraft is a psychic act arising from his or her innate power to do harm [89; 45]. Valid or not for Africa, this distinction cannot be translated to Europe or North America. Here there was little practical distinction made between sorcerer and witch, and although it is true that Scottish dittays (indictments) very often charged the accused with acts of sorcery and witchcraft as though the two were different activities, the likelihood is that the formula was little more than legal verbosity. In common usage, then, 'sorcerer' tended to amalgamate its original meaning of 'diviner' with 'practitioner of largely harmful magic' and thus 'witch'. The point may be illustrated by the title given to the 1575 English translation of an essay on witchcraft by the French Calvinist, Lambert Daneau: *A Dialogue of Witches in Foretime named Lot-tellers and now commonly called Sorcerers* [see further **108**].

Now, magic in the northern hemisphere was seen as manifesting itself principally in specific acts accompanied by words, as one may observe, for example, from paragraph 44 of the 1532 law code of

Emperor Charles V, which refers to 'gestures, words, and signs such as characterise sorcery'. In the case of ceremonial magicians (exclusively male), these might be learned or read from a book; but in the case of witches (largely female), it is probable they were learned from oral tradition, whether within or outwith the immediate family, unless, of course, they were improvised for the occasion. Most European and North American magic and witchcraft therefore would fall under the Africans' general definition of sorcery. One exception, of course, was the influence and use of the evil eye (*fascinatio*), for anyone possessed of such a characteristic (*qualitas* in Latin) had only to look at someone or something to effect a transfer of malevolence or envy which would then usually manifest itself in the form of disease or loss of power [41;76]. Increase Mather, for example, recorded that during the Salem witch-trials the magistrates and ministers present bore witness that when a certain child 'did but cast its Eye upon the afflicted Persons, they were tormented; and they held her Head, and yet so many as her Eye could fix upon were afflicted'. It is difficult to tell whether or not a second exception can be found in the *guérisseur*, the curer who was believed to possess a secret which enabled him or her to cure a specific disease or group of diseases. This secret, if one may extrapolate from eighteenth- and nineteenth-century evidence, might consist of words or gestures or both, which could be passed on by the curer to someone else – an operation thus learned and not transmitted by blood. But there is also the suggestion that some *guérisseurs* had a gift rather than a secret, which would imply the existence of some innate curative quality in his or her person, which enabled any magical words or actions to operate with effect. *Fascinatio*, however, undoubtedly did present such a phenomenon and it is not surprising, therefore, to find that doctors were especially interested in it, and from the fifteenth century onwards wrote treatises seeking to explain it in other than purely theological terms [124, 30, 50–3].

Scholars usually subdivided magic into three broad categories: (a) natural, (b) deceptive and (c) demonic.

Natural Magic concerned itself largely with investigating the occult relationships between every part of creation and then exploiting or manipulating them to produce novel effects or useful inventions and processes. An Italian physician, Giambattista della Porta, described natural magic as 'the practical part of natural philosophy', and a glance at the contents of his book, *Natural Magic* (1558), gives a very good notion of what he meant by this. Beginning with a discussion of the hidden laws of creation, he goes on to talk about the generation of animals and new plants, advice on good house-keeping, alchemy, counterfeiting precious stones, natural magnet-ism, strange cures, cosmetics, distillation, perfumes, gunpowder and other explosive or flaming devices, tempering steel, cookery, fishing, hunting, invisible writing, experiments with lenses, weight, air, ending his book with a miscellany of experiments. Little or none of this is what we would recognise as 'magic', although della Porta's underlying presumptions are those of the magical universe. This is magic as 'science' and was generally regarded as an acceptable form of the art, qualified approval or tolerance being contingent upon what the experimenter was trying to achieve and how he was trying to achieve it.

Deceptive Magic included the arts of deliberate illusion and what today would be called 'conjuring'. In 1437, Johann Nider recorded several examples.

> At Cologne, a young girl was summoned to appear in court. She had been performing remarkable things, apparently by magic, in front of an audience of the nobility. It was said she had ripped a napkin to pieces and suddenly put it back together again in full view of everyone. She threw a glass at a wall. It broke and instantly she repaired it.   (*Formicarius*, c.1476)

People were well aware that such tricks could be done by sleight of hand, and the girl was probably arrested so that the authorities could check she was accomplishing her feats without the help of any evil spirit. Since we are told that the Inquisition took no interest in her case, we may assume she was able to prove her 'conjuring' was natural.

The older sense of 'conjuring', however, did indeed refer to the summoning of evil spirits, and it was their presence and assistance which characterised Demonic Magic. So all kinds of magical opera-tions, even if they were beneficial in intent, might be rendered suspicious by the possibility that the operator had entered explicitly or implicitly into some kind of pact with Satan, renouncing his or her baptism, faith in and duty to Jesus Christ and hope of salvation, in return for demonic aid which would lend some kind of power to the magician's ritual words and actions and so enable the magic to work, that is, achieve the magician's purpose. Curing the sick, divination, spells for love, finding buried treasure, and a host of other desirable intentions apparently not achievable by natural means already known to and approved by legitimate authority, might mask just such a diabolical covenant, and in consequence came under the apprehensive, cautious eye of the Church and through her the eye of the state as well. A magician's intention to do magical harm to others or their property self-evidently could be taken to imply the existence of this pact, and since witchcraft was always considered to involve deliberate *maleficium*, it is clear that scholarly writers were likely to interpret witchcraft quite simply as a form of demonic magic.

Learned writers also became increasingly concerned to locate all forms of magic within the natural world and explain them by reference either to deliberate deception on someone's part or to the operation of occult (i.e. secret) laws and relationships which might eventually be discovered or revealed. Their aim was to draw people away from the ever-present dangerous tendency to attribute too much independent power to Satan and so set him up as a kind of rival to God, a Manichaeism which always seemed to underlie popular attitudes to and beliefs about magic. Hence the Jesuit Martin Del Rio's definition: 'Magic can be defined very loosely, and in a way which will be universally acceptable, as "an art or skill which, by the use of natural, *not* supernatural, power accomplishes extraordinary and unusual things".'

Witchcraft

Given this fluidity of understanding and experience of the various kinds of magic, one's inclination is to assume that a good way to come to an understanding of what people understood by 'witchcraft' in particular is to look at statute law and the ways people responded to it. Since the law requires definitional precision, and intending prosecutors must perforce be able to accuse their suspects of a specific offence, it is surely reasonable to expect that in practice witchcraft will tend to be whatever the law says it is. Those drafting the law will, of course, bear in mind and be influenced by the pronouncements of theologians, custom and legal precedents. Nevertheless, without statute definition there is no crime to prosecute.

Yet it is a curious fact that the statutes do not seem to offer any definition of 'witchcraft' at all. Usually they refer either to the types of people who are to be condemned under the provisions of the law, such as we see in the *Theodosian Code* which proscribes the work of 'the Chaldaeans and wizards and all the rest of those the common people call magicians'; or they mention a variety of magical operations as, for example, the Scottish Witchcraft Act of 1563 which speaks of 'the heavy and abominable superstition used by divers lieges of this realm by using of witchcrafts, sorcery, and necromancy'; or the earlier English statute of 1542 which introduces itself as 'the bill against conjurations and witchcrafts and sorcery and enchantments', with which one may compare the wording of Louis XIV's edict of 1682 with its references to 'maléfices, empoisonnements, sacrilèges et sorcelleries'. So, in the absence of any specific legal definition of what constituted 'witchcraft', judges and juries were left to decide for themselves – within the obvious intentions apparent or inherent in their local or national statute – how to interpret the acts of the accused appearing before them.

They knew, of course, the kind of intent and action which would tend to classify an act of magic as 'witchcraft', for they were guided by their own expectation of finding certain characteristics. Apart from the well-known theological or demonological speculations about witches' flying through the air to a Sabbat, worshipping the Devil there, or carrying Satan's marks on their body, these amounted to three. One was the presence of at least one example of *maleficium*, 'an act of harmful magic' – a major (perhaps *the* major) trait for which they were looking. Another was the witch's intention in performing his or her magical operation, and Roman and canon law especially looked for evidence of this maleficent intention, tending to limit criminal liability to those cases in which it could be proved [72]. Hence the force behind Jean Bodin's definition of a witch as 'someone who *knowingly* tries to accomplish something by diabolical means'.

A third we have met already: the existence of some kind of pact between the operator and Satan or one of his evil spirits, a pact which had been described by Saint Augustine as having the nature of a private, commercial contract, the terms of which had special significance for both magician and evil spirit. This pact quickly assumed a compelling importance in any official investigation of suspect witches because the range of magical acts which were presented to the authorities for their consideration was not uniform in being evil or having necessarily evil intent. Witches were believed not only to work harm but also to perform magical cures on behalf of sick animals or people, make one person fall in love with another, divine the future, find lost objects, and relieve the suffering of someone enduring the *maleficium* of another witch, and it was always possible that in some cases at least, the magic could be deemed to depend upon natural rather than demonic causes. But if it was decided that a diabolic pact, whether explicit or implicit, lay behind the operation, then that magical act could be designated 'witchcraft', something which can be seen in the witchcraft statutes of several of the New England colonies, wherein a witch is defined as a person 'that hath or consulteth with a familiar spirit'.

Judges, then, or juries, or indeed people faced by evidence of magic in everyday life, were faced by a problem of interpretation, a problem exacerbated by the fact that the crime called 'witchcraft' usually included a number of activities such as apostasy, heresy, murder, destruction of crops and animals, infanticide and adultery, which were themselves indictable. The extra dimension added, in the case of witchcraft, to crimes such as these, and the one which bound any or all of them together, was the perpetrator's suspected ability to accomplish them by means of magic. So people, whether those of official status or not, had to try to decide that either the person suspected of witchcraft could exercise an ambiguous preternatural power which he or she could use according to personal intention for good or ill in relation to herself or others; or that her good witchcraft could be interpreted as being fundamentally malevolent, regardless of its apparent benefits and harmlessness, simply because one was likely to assume the existence of a diabolical pact. Hence, of course, accused witches were not the only magical operators to fall under this suspicion. Cunning folk, who specialised in the beneficial applications of magic, usually for curing illness or lifting other people's *maleficium*, were as likely as witches to be tried and condemned for witchcraft. For it was argued that in as much as the cunning folk misled their clients into sin with a pretence of doing good by relying upon an explicit or implicit partnership with the Devil, they were actually greater deceivers than witches and therefore even more to be deprecated and condemned. As Henry Howard said: 'There is not one among them to be founde that worketh any good, no not one, theyre throate is an open sepulchre, and theyr steppes leade to hell'; and the English Puritan theologian William Perkins neatly summed up the situation as follows:

By Witches we understand not those onely which kill and torment: but all Diviners, Charmers, Juglers, all Wizzards, commonly called wise men and wise women; yea, whosoever doe any thing (knowing what they doe) which cannot be effected by nature or art; and in the same number we reckon all good Witches, which doe no hurt but good, which doe not spoile and destroy, but save and deliver.

(*A Discourse of the Damned Art of Witchcraft*, 1609)

The common people tended to agree. As far as they were concerned, divisions and categories were little more than a literary and scholarly construct evolved for the sake of learned argument. If the authorities were more interested in the existence of a diabolic pact and the more sensational aspects of what one is tempted to call 'official' witchcraft, everyone else was principally concerned with malefice: had the accused wilfully and intentionally tried to work harmful magic against his or her neighbours? Moreover, to everyday man and woman, magic, sorcery, and witchcraft could easily seem to be similar kinds of activity, ebbing and flowing the one into the other according to local and individual circumstance, and greeted with popular approval or disapproval for just the same reasons, so that someone such as Reginald Scot was able to say: 'at this daie it is indifferent to saie in the English toong, she is a witch or she is a wise woman', and Latin–English dictionaries could define *saga* as 'a witch, a sorceresse, a wife or subtill woman' (Thomas Thomas, *Dictionarium*, 1587), and *magia* as 'naturall magic, also witchcrafte, southsayinge, sorserie' (Thomas Cooper, *Thesaurus*, 1565). Hence official nervousness at the sight of magic steering dangerously close to heterodox religious beliefs, and hence the tendency of this same officialdom to amalgamate the activities of witches and cunning-folk.

Concluding Remarks

Witchcraft, therefore, did not refer to some well-defined, universal system of magical belief or behaviour but to a complex interdependency of local beliefs and practices which might, under certain, locally influenced circumstances, be interpreted as witchcraft and brought to court as such; and throughout the whole period of its existence in a community it would pass through several layers of scrutiny and interpretation. Members of that community would constantly be asking themselves whether such and such an act constituted 'witchcraft', and if so whether they wanted to have it prosecuted. Officialdom in the shape of lawyers, doctors and clergy would try to decide whether the acts brought to their attention constituted prosecutable witchcraft or owed more to physical sickness, psychological disturbance, fraud, personal malice or a dozen other possible motives or causes. At some point, demonological theory might be taken into account and the expectations of learned discourse brought to bear on the details of an individual case. Should the magical operator find him- or herself in court, the judge or jury would have to consider whether or not the acts presented to them constituted punishable witchcraft according to the relevant statute; and in some cases political considerations might also play a part in the way the available evidence was assessed [114; 108]. Nothing could be further from some hegemonising totalitarian reaction to witches and witchcraft on the part of authority. Rather, ambiguous complexity forms the keynote of Mediaeval and early modern dealings with the whole subject. As Ruggiero has put it, witchcraft can be seen as 'a broad, rather empty conceptual frame of fear with certain points of reference like the Sabbat ... but with large areas free to be filled in with ... anxieties and discontents' [118, 231]. Underlying them, however, there would always be three fundamental expectations which would be likely to render any act of magic interpretable as 'witchcraft': (a) the intention to do harm by preternatural means, (b) an actual deed wrought by means of harmful magic, and (c) an alliance of some kind between the magical practitioner and an evil spirit.

2

Late Mediaeval Attitudes to Witchcraft

Miracles and Marvels

One of the distinguishing characteristics of the Middle Ages was their capacity for astonishment (*admiratio*), a complexity of emotions which might range from terror and dread to enchantment and delight. In Callois's vivid phrase, they bathed in the marvellous. So embracing was this capacity that it took a while even for scholars to begin to distinguish between a miracle and a marvel. Caesarius of Heisterbach, a Cistercian monk writing in the early thirteenth century, for example, defined a miracle as 'whatever is done contrary to the usual course of nature'. This universal embracement, however, proved unsatisfactory for later theologians, not to mention demonologists, and we find St Thomas Aquinas providing what was to be regarded as the essential distinction between the two. A miracle, he said, is an unusual happening, both sublime and difficult to comprehend, which is produced by the power of God alone, whereas a marvel is simply a natural effect we fail to understand (*Questions About the Power of God*, 6). But this is a distinction which, however accurate, was likely to have escaped most people during the Middle Ages. For them there might be little discernible difference between a cure worked by a saint through his or her relic and a cure worked by a magical *guérisseur*. Both merited astonishment and both would almost certainly be received with equal gratitude.

The simple fact is, most people were not intellectually under the effective control of theological or legal speculation. Nice distinctions may have been important for the learned, but for everyone else a cure was a cure was a cure. The priest of Ramsholt, indeed, tried to cure his daughter by magical means before he tried praying to St Thomas Becket for a miracle; in June 1171 the monks of Canterbury had to defend themselves against accusations that they were themselves accomplishing St Thomas's cures by working magic; and pilgrims to his shrine at Canterbury wore ampoules of his curative water round their necks in just the same way as they would wear magical amulets. [46, *62–3*; 40, *266–87*]. Christian prayers, particularly the 'Our Father', regularly accompanied attempts to achieve healing, and verses from the Gospel of St John were copied out and worn for magical protection as were the blessed wax images known as *agnus Dei*; and it was a fine distinction, (since the difference between them was scarcely noticeable) between this type of remedy which was permitted and approved by the Church, and others she declared superstitious and illegitimate.

To be fair, however, one must remember that it is common experience for people, and indeed institutions, to live their lives on several different levels without necessarily being conscious that they are doing so. They can therefore accommodate different and even contradictory beliefs, one coming to the fore at one time, another at another. Thus, despite official Christian disapproval and condemnation of magical activities and beliefs, a Bohemian priest was found to be carrying an umbilical cord in his bag to ward off an unpleasant death, Russian clergy were often the employers of spells (*zagovory*) designed to protect, exorcise or do harm to others, and all over Western Christendom priests regularly said Mass over an extraordinary variety of objects concealed beneath the cloths over their altars with a view to enchanting them or imbuing them with preternatural power. Indeed, from the *grimoires* (books of spells) of both Mediaeval and early modern times one gets the firm impression that there may have been scarcely a church anywhere which did not have its quota of curious, would-be magical objects lurking beneath the altar cloth; and, in fact, so deeply were the clergy involved in such consecrations, that at least one modern scholar has been able to write of the existence of a whole clerical sub-culture of magic coexistent with that of the laity [67, *153–6*; 121, *167*].

So the Mediaeval theologian or lawyer or doctor might retire to his study and thence produce learned dissertations upon the exact relationships between magic and miracle, marvel, witchcraft and science, condemning many widespread practices as no better than foolish superstition. These lucubrations he might then publish for the benefit and instruction of the small audience capable of understanding them: men, in other words, such as himself. But the majority of people denied access, for whatever reason (be it educational insufficiency or personal indifference), to his studies, pursued their own ways more or less regardless, although preachers, who provided one of the few regular points of contact between learned and popular culture during this period, might have a profound, if temporary, effect. The obvious example is St Bernardino of Siena who frequently thundered against any form of popular magic. His most famous sermon, delivered on 15 August, 1427, warned his Sienese listeners to shun the use of charms and those who proffered them. He took as his principal theme the trial and execution of two witches in Rome not long before and the sermon he had preached there for the occasion. The effect on his auditors was so great, he said, that in spite of their initial disbelief that such wickedness as he described was possible, they quickly realised he was speaking the truth, and proceeded to denounce a large number of women who confessed to horrendous crimes including murder, shape-changing and worshipping the Devil. Such people, declared St Bernardino, should be burned without compunction, and he strongly hinted that he would like to see the Roman experience repeated in Siena [**96**, *52–108*].

Signs of the Times

Neither magic nor witchcraft existed in a vacuum. The fourteenth and fifteenth centuries, which began to see notable changes in the way witchcraft in particular was regarded by both ecclesiastical and secular authorities, initiated a period of increasing psychological disturbance as learned and unlearned alike witnessed the devastations wrought by the Black Death, an apparent burgeoning of heresy under various guises, and the dislocation of the Papacy from Rome to Avignon from 1308 to 1378 – and at the same time waited in expectation of the end of the world, the closure of time, the birth of Antichrist and the second coming of Jesus. The Bible was graphic in its description of the last days. 'The day of the Lord shall come as a thief in the night; in which the heavens shall pass away with a great noise, and the elements shall melt with fervent heat, the earth also and the works that are therein shall be burned up' (2 Peter 3: 10).

These terrors naturally precipitated a desire to know exactly what they meant and when humanity could expect them to arrive, and to the latter at least St John gave an important clue. For he said that Satan had been bound in chains and cast into a bottomless pit, there to languish for a thousand years, after which he would be released for a while to wreak havoc in the world until Christ came again and disposed of him for ever. His short period of freedom would be announced by the birth of Antichrist, either an incarnation of Satan himself or a creature entirely controlled by him.

When would Antichrist appear? When could one expect the end of the world to begin? Again and again calculations and expectations failed. In 1033 there was widespread famine and plague in Europe, taken to be a signal of the end. In 1095 Pope Urban II preached the first crusade as a preliminary to preparing Christendom for the last great battle with Antichrist. A Cistercian mystic, Joachim of Fiore, in a series of complex prophecies, suggested this would begin in 1260. Mindful of the prediction made in Matthew 24: 29, Jacopone da Todi wrote bleakly in the late 1290s that Antichrist would be coming very soon: 'The tribulations which have been foretold, I see them menacing from every direction'. The Black Death of 1348–50 was taken by many to herald the end; in 1379 the English heretic Wycliffe declared that Antichrist had already arrived, and identified him as the reigning Pope. So did the Czech, Jan Huss. A conjunction of Jupiter and Saturn in 1484 was seen by astrologers as significant of the end, and throughout the late 1480s and early 1490s the Dominican Savonarola preached to the people of Florence the imminence of God's kingdom. Only Cardinal Pierre d'Ailly seemed to offer a crumb of comfort. Writing in 1414, he predicted astrologically that Antichrist would not be coming until 1789 [83; 148].

Witchcraft and Heresy

The increasing terrors of the time thus played their part in creating an atmosphere in which persons or groups who deviated too far from the accepted norms laid down by both ecclesiastical and secular authority were likely to run an increased risk of persecution – as may be seen, for example, from anti-Jewish pogroms in 1348, stimulated by the Black Death and underlining a trend evident from the late thirteenth century for close association of the Jews with witchcraft, poison and various kinds of maleficent magic [48]. The Church, indeed, began to see herself as a city under siege, called upon to defend the true faith from a bewildering variety of Satanic assaults while the Last Days drew near. Ecclesiastics of all kinds frequently found themselves the objects of murderous hatred as anticlerical prophecies of mayhem proliferated during the thirteenth and fourteenth centuries, thus reinforcing a siege mentality in the ruling élites and inducing a keen suspicion among them of any manifestations of unorthodoxy by the poor and uneducated. Jews, therefore, while falling under this suspicion, were by no means as potentially frightening as heretics; and since heretics both could be and were viewed as allies of Satan in the war against Antichrist, it was always possible that heresy would be linked with magic to form a relatively new and lethal offence against orthodox society.

This we can see happening in the case of an heretical group, begun in c.1170 by Peter Waldo, calling itself 'the Poor of Lyons' and known by others as 'Waldensians' or 'Vaudois' after its founder. These people started to exercise the Church's particular attention during the early fifteenth century. The reason seems to have been that between 1438 and 1461 several persons in Fribourg and Arras were arrested and executed on charges of *vauderie*, by which the officials meant 'witchcraft', and so, by little more than semantic shift, a community of heretics became identified with a diabolically-inspired conspiracy against the Church, and indeed the whole of Christian society.

During the course of this shift a number of significant details of *Vaudois* behaviour emerged. The accused made an ointment and smeared it upon a small wooden stick which they then placed between their legs and so were enabled to fly. They attended a witches' convention (the *Sabbat*) during which they feasted, profaned a crucifix, worshipped the Devil and took part in a sexual orgy: thus the inquisitor Lebrousse in a sermon preached on the day of their execution, 9 May 1460. Some of these details were not new. Bartolo da Sassoferrato (c.1314–c.1357), for example, the most influential jurist of his time, had written of an accused witch that she confessed to having made a cross in order to trample upon it, had worshipped the Devil and had murdered children by touching them or infecting them by means of her evil eye. The flight through the air, however, seems to have been derived from an even earlier tradition recorded in the Canon Episcopi, a piece of canon law dating from c.906., which, one should note, actually regarded the notion with a degree of scepticism.

Some wicked women, turn themselves round to face the other way behind Satan and, led astray by hallucinations and figments of their imaginations created by evil spirits, believe and maintain that during the hours of night they ride upon certain beasts along with Diana (a goddess of the pagans), or with Herodias and an innumerable host of women, traversing many areas of the earth in the silent dead of night; that they obey her commands as though she were their mistress, and that on specific nights they are called to her service.

The reference to the women's facing the opposite direction of travel is interesting because this inversion can be seen in fifteenth- and sixteenth-century woodcuts and paintings of witches in flight. But from the beginning, belief in such a flight aroused both scepticism and acceptance.

On the one hand, we have Johannes Nider, a German Dominican and one of the most important early writers on witchcraft, and one who described aspects of the 'new' witchcraft several decades before this reinterpretation became an official norm. His *Formicarius* (Ant Heap) was published at some point between 1435 and 1437, and its aim was to edify believers and develop a comparison between the society of ants and that of human beings. It is therefore not directly addressed to witchcraft, but its fifth part describes the malefices of *maleficii* (people of either sex who work harmful magic), and may have been based, at least in part, on prosecutions for witchcraft in Simmental in about 1400, since he knew the lay judge in the cases, Peter von Greyerz. These malefices include destroying a neighbour's harvest by sacrificing a black hen to an evil spirit who then calls up the requested storm, killing and eating children, (thirteen altogether), paying homage to evil spirits, and recognising as 'little master' of the witches a dominant evil spirit who is never actually called 'the Devil' and may not necessarily have been him.

Most interestingly, perhaps, Nider also says a Dominican friar (he may mean himself), along with several other men, was an eye-witness to the flight of a witch to a Sabbat (which is always called a 'synagogue' at this period, a reminder of the anti-Semitism which was rife at the time). She smeared herself with ointment in his presence, pronounced various magical formulae, and then appeared to fall into a deep sleep. It lasted for a long time during which she moved her arms and legs and gave many deep sighs, and when she woke she said she had flown to her Sabbat, a detailed description of which follows in Nider's account. Nider, one may note, calls the woman 'deranged' and characterises her belief as 'bad faith' or 'falsehood'. It is also worth noting that the anecdote owes nothing to Greek or Latin sources but is based on what purports to be a personal experience. This imparts, or at least is intended to impart, verisimilitude and authenticity, and fulfils a function of similar anecdotes (*historiae*) which bulk large in all the demonologies of this and later periods, that is, to raise *admiratio* in the reader or listener and emphasise the difference between him, a member of the orthodox, 'normal' community, and them, deluded or willing participants on Satan's side in the battle between good and evil.

Contemporary with this, in about 1436, after having been actively engaged in the prosecution of witches, Claude Tholosan, a judge from Dauphiné, decided to publish an account of his juridic experiences. In this, *Ut magorum et maleficiorum errores* (The Errors of Magicians and Workers of Harmful Magic), he shows himself quite opposed to the notion of a witch's flight through the air or the reality of the Sabbat, but discusses in detail what he sees as a sect directed by the Devil, which is given to denial of Christ and the ritual practice of apostasy and idolatry. He thus accentuated the heretical elements in witchcraft but, having done so, goes on to explain that the secular prince, 'who knows no superior' and is the repository of God's justice, has a special duty in regard to this particular crime. So Tholosan takes the question of witchcraft beyond (but not, of course, out of) the hands of clerics, and encourages his readers to see the state as having a special concern in seeing witchcraft uprooted from civil society.

In c.1440, Alonso Tostado, Bishop of Avila, answered his own question, 'Can people sometimes be transported by the Devil through various places?' with a round assertive: 'Evil spirits can sometimes cause people to move through various places by day as well as by night, sometimes willingly and sometimes against their will', (*Commentary on Matthew*, question 47); and *Le Champion des Dames*, written by Martin le Franc in 1440–2, draws together several of these various themes. Le Franc was secretary to the anti-Pope Felix V at the Council of Basel and Provost of the chapter of Lausanne from 1443. His book, written in verse, is cast in the form of a dispute between a Champion and his Adversary who offers us a description of 'good witches' who fly on sticks to their synagogue where they meet the Devil to whom they offer homage. The Adversary goes on to give details of cannibalism, sexual orgies, malefices, apostasy, and the metamorphosis of the Devil into an animal. The Champion in his turn, however, takes the women's part and refuses to believe that any of this can be true, especially the flight through the air.

Finally, one is offered by other writers on the subject a kind of compromise. Martin of Arles, for example, denied that an evil spirit can actually move witches from one place to another. Rather, he said, Satan seizes upon a woman's weakness of faith and misleads her into thinking that the phantasmagoric images and likenesses he puts into her mind while she is asleep are real, so that she genuinely believes she has ridden with Diana or Venus and committed all kinds of wicked deeds (*Tractatus de superstitionibus*, c.1515).

Learned debate, however, did not always produce a guarded scepticism. For example, an anonymous tract of c.1450, *Errores Gazariorum* (The Errors of Witches), which may well have been written by an inquisitor on the basis of confessions he had heard during the course of his interrogations of heretics in Savoy, gives a detailed description of what happened during a witches' Sabbat.

The Enemy appears sometimes in the form of a black cat, sometimes in the form of an imperfect human or in the likeness of some other animal: but usually in the likeness of a black cat. The person who has been brought to the Sabbat is then asked by the Devil whether he wants to become a permanent member of the society and obey the least command of the one who had fetched him thither, and he replies that he does. At this, the Devil exacts an oath of fidelity from him..... . Once he has promised to keep his oath, the wretched, deceived man worships the president of the assembly and does him homage; and as a sign of homage, he kisses the Devil (who appears in human or, as I said earlier, some other form) upon the 'arse' or anus, and gives him a part of his body after death by way of tribute. Then all the members of that noxious sect hurry to express their pleasure at the arrival of the new heretic, recommending to him those things which belong to them, especially the dead children who have been boiled and roasted. When the accursed dinner is finished and everyone has danced as much as he or she wishes, the Devil (who is presiding at the time) calls out, 'Mingle, mingle', and the light is extinguished. At the sound of his voice, each person has sexual intercourse with someone else, male with female, male with male, and sometimes father with daughter, son with mother, brother with sister, without the least observance of the natural order.... The light is rekindled; once again they eat and drink, and then when they leave the table they urinate and defecate into large earthenware pots. When you ask them why they do this, they say they do it in contempt and scorn of the sacrament of the eucharist.

Several points are worth noting. The writer refers to the assembly as a 'sect', a religious term indicating his opinion that the witches form a coherent, unorthodox body given over to the worship of Satan, thereby committing the sins of idolatry and apostasy. There are men present as well as women. The various words for 'witch' did not come to be associated almost exclusively with women until later, and this mixture of the sexes can be seen in contemporary trials. In March 1448, for example, the Inquisition interrogated several people of various social ranks about their claims to have gone to a Sabbat where they met Satan, made a pact with him, indulged in sexual orgies, and ate the flesh of children [103]; and between the summer of 1477 and the spring of 1484, seven men and women were questioned under torture about their alleged membership of a diabolic sect, attending Sabbats, renouncing God, worshipping the Devil under the form of a black cat, and eating children's flesh [85; 1]. In fact, as Borst has pointed out, 'almost everywhere in early Alpine witchcraft, it was men who dominated; not until the late fifteenth century did the fear of witches concentrate on women and on the suspicion of sexual orgies' [21].

The horror stories which appear in these accounts of witches have a long history. Minucius Felix, a Christian of the second or third century, recorded some of the common pagan charges against Christians, one of which maintained that they would meet in secret at night, kill a baby and then lick its blood as part of an initiatory rite, and on special feast-days after dinner would cause the light to be extinguished and then indulge in random copulation during which no distinction of sex age, or consanguinity was observed or mattered (*Octavius* 9:5–7). Closer to home, the list of accusations against the Templars in 1308 charged them with meeting in secret, spitting upon the cross, kissing the presiding officer on various parts of the body including the anus, and worshipping Satan under the guise of an idol called 'Baphomet' [80; 104]. As for the witches' flight, Ginzburg has pointed out its precedents in widespread folk-beliefs which had nothing to do specifically with witches (*Ecstasies*, Penguin Books, 1992).

Europe at this time, one must remember, was not the monolithic Roman Christian entity of myth and popular assumption. Large tracts of it had scarcely been converted more than skin-deep, whole areas were still to all intents and purposes pagan, and since the purpose of the missionaries was to win over pagans from both their native religions and their magical practices, there was a tendency to run paganism and magic together and treat them as though they were more or less one and the same [47; 90]. Nevertheless, official views and interpretations of popular beliefs and practices remained relatively fluid for a while, as can be seen from learned debate over witches' ability to fly. But during the fourteenth century in particular official attitudes were beginning to harden, and it would not be long before Church and state would decide that in magic they were faced by an adversary not so much eccentric as hostile. The principal reason is straightforward. The concept of a demonic pact was being grafted on to popular magical practices and this changed them fundamentally from being private acts done for personal advantage or malicious gratification to potential assaults upon the foundations of Church and state [8]. Officialdom and 'the rest' were, in fact, drawing apart and as they did so 'the rest' became inclined to feel themselves distinct from the Church in particular both in what they were willing to believe and in what they were unwilling to surrender. Hence a growth in ecclesiastical hostility to and censure of opinions and practices which were increasingly designated 'heretical'.

Witches and the Law

One should not lose sight of the fact that throughout Europe witches were brought to court on criminal charges and were tried according to law. They were not, except in a few isolated instances, the victims of lynching or crowd hysteria [78; 63]. The procedures used by the criminal courts during the sixteenth and seventeenth centuries, however, were not those which had existed earlier in the Europe of the thirteenth century. Up to that point, bringing an accusation and seeing it through the criminal process lay in the hands of the individual who believed he or she had suffered wrong. Known as 'the accusatorial system', it depended for its success upon the accused's making a confession of guilt, undeniable proof of guilt furnished by the accuser, or testing by ordeal.

This last was, in effect, an appeal to God to demonstrate the guilt or innocence of the accused by working a miracle. Ordeal by fire, for example, required the accused to hold or walk on red-hot iron for a specified time or distance; ordeal by water meant immersing the hand in boiling water, or being swum in a pool or stream. God, it was maintained, would heal in a very short time the damage done by the heat, and in the case of the ordeal by pool would not permit an innocent person to drown when he or she sank to the bottom [10, 13–24].

But in 1215, the Fourth Lateran Council forbade clerics from taking part in any future ordeals and this effectively meant that secular courts would either have to conduct these judicial appeals to God without the participation of the Church or forego the use of ordeals as part of their regular criminal process. Increasing sophistication of legal theory and procedure sustained, as it had perhaps initiated, these changes and gradually the ordeal began to fall into disuse. Floating the accused, however, continued to be practised in the case of magical practitioners, (perhaps because a close association was made between witchcraft and heresy, the water of the pool or stream and the water of baptism), and the practice, though diminishing, did not entirely die out until the nineteenth century.

Other possibilities of proving innocence or guilt under this system had the accused or proxy fight a duel, this trial by combat demonstrating his innocence or guilt according to whether he won or lost the contest; or he might swear his innocence and have the oath confirmed by the co-swearing of a number of people willing to bear testimony this way on his or her behalf. It is evident, therefore, that the accusatorial system tended to favour the accused since it had a tendency to depend on theatrical demonstration rather than cool inquiry into fact and circumstance; and the standard of proof required to establish guilt was extraordinarily high, 'clearer than the midday light', as the saying went [25]. Moreover, should the accuser fail to make his case, he himself was liable to find himself in court for bringing a malicious prosecution.

So these considerations, and the fact that the system was neither efficient nor in tune with legal development from the thirteenth century onwards, meant that a change was bound to happen. Gradually a new way of proceeding replaced it. Known as 'the inquisitorial system', it derived from Roman law. Accusation could be made by a private individual, by a community acting as a single complainant, or by judicial officers relying upon information received; but once the accusation had been initiated, it was court officials who investigated the alleged crime, interrogated witnesses, recorded statements, evaluated the evidence, and came to a decision about the accused's guilt or innocence. The system was widely adopted throughout Europe, although two countries decided not to follow the model. Scotland adapted it by having a jury decide and pronounce a verdict at the end of the trial, while having court officers assemble the written evidence as described above. England, on the other hand, resisted adoption of the new system altogether and clung to its own version of the accusatorial procedure.

The result of these changes is clear. The accuser stood much less chance of finding him-or herself charged with malice in the event of the accused's being found not guilty, so it was psychologically easier to make an accusation; and investigation of the alleged crime was much more rigorous, and conducted according to rules which were intended to help the interrogator elicit the truth. Hence, the accused had a more difficult task if he or she wanted to prove or demonstrate innocence. But there were problems for the court. Proof depended entirely upon a confession by the accused or the sworn testimony of at least two eye-witnesses to the crime. Now obviously most acts of witchcraft were done in secret, so the evidence of eye-witnesses would be very difficult to obtain, and hearsay evidence was not admissible. Hence torture entered the proceedings and although the rules governing its application were very strict in theory, (and one is not entitled to assume that torture was used wholesale on every person arrested on a charge of witchcraft), nevertheless the rules were frequently abused and in consequence a large number of miscarriages of justice is bound to have occurred. To some extent, therefore, the change in the judicial system can be said to have encouraged an increase in the number of accusations of witchcraft and many of their subsequent guilty verdicts [78, 64–8].

Concluding Remarks

Two general conceptions of witchcraft can be detected as the fourteenth century gave way to the fifteenth. The first encompasses the beliefs and practices of ritual and popular magic, including acts of malefice, invocation of spirits, and so forth, all of which were common before the beginning of the fifteenth century. But then one can see official notions of witchcraft gliding towards combining them with, or designating them as, heresy pure and simple. Thus a relatively novel stereotype of the witch began to emerge as one who had entered into a formal pact with the Devil, practised murder, infanticide, cannibalism, sodomy and bestiality during the course of Satanic meetings, and deliberately surrendered to the demands of apostasy. Hence in the early part of the fifteenth century there flourished writings which attest to the emergence of this new picture, of which Nider's *Formicarius*, parts of Le Franc's *Champion des Dames* and the anonymous *Errores Gazariorum* are prime examples.

For the fact is that during the fifteenth century, various pressures were combining to demonise magic and turn much of it into apparent manifestations of a pact, explicit or implicit, between the magical operator and a Satan whose time of freedom from ancient bondage had either arrived or was about to happen as a prelude to the Last Days and a final struggle between the forces of good and evil. In consequence, the older attitude of official disapproval allied to effectual toleration of many popular beliefs and practices began to break down, while ecclesiastical writers in particular tried to grapple with formulation and explanation of official reasons for condemning and more actively prosecuting those people who clung to old, unorthodox, and sometimes not even Christian occult operations. Sometimes these attempts discovered themselves in the form of intellectual debate, as in scholarly disagreements over the reality of the Sabbat or the witches' flight thither; sometimes, as Ginzburg has shown, officials simply misunderstood or reinterpreted folk beliefs to make them coincide with official preconceptions (*Night Battles*, London, 1983).

Nor were the accused always those who had allegedly taken part in Sabbats. Magical curers and diviners were equally liable to be accused of the same kind of heresy (idolatry and apostasy) during the later decades of the fifteenth century; and as official reformulation of what constituted witchcraft entered popular mentality via sermons, court verdicts and the whole theatre of public executions, so there came into being the ever-increasing possibility that common folk would perceive what officials meant by 'witchcraft' and be the readier, when it came to accusing someone of it and bearing witness in court, to translate popular understanding into terms which would be understand by and acceptable to the authorities in the case [17]. Something of the kind can be seen, for example, in many Scottish witchcraft cases where it is clear that the accused was claiming to have met and had dealings with fairies, but that the court (whether ecclesiastical or criminal) was choosing to reinterpret this as traffic with evil spirits and therefore recognisable 'witchcraft'.

At the basis, then, the vagaries and formulations of official opinion boiled down to arguments about the precise extent of Satan's power in this world; the nature of that power (whether real or illusory); how far, if real, it might be permitted by God himself to encroach upon divine omnipotence; and for what reasons God would allow Satan to impose, either in illusion or in reality, upon the rest of creation.

3

Two Influential Witchcraft Treatises

Preliminary Remarks

Authority, whether secular or religious, had always been suspicious of magical activity even while individual members of bodies exercising authority had themselves been willing to work magic on their own behalf or for other people. The principal consideration which caused official wrath tended to be the use of magic to do harm, the *maleficium* of legal and theological documents. But during the fifteenth century in particular, learned opinion was piecing together a set of theories which would describe what witches were supposed to do and thus, by implication, provide a loose definition of what constituted witchcraft, although this last was open to wide interpretation according to which parts of the official theory were accepted or questioned by local judges and juries. 'Witchcraft' thus started to look like two rather different operations. One consisted of a set of activities described in learned demonological literature; the other of the collected perceptions of non-learned individuals who either used or denounced the witch in accordance with transitory and particular circumstances.

Now, I am not here resurrecting the old notion of élite versus popular culture, for everyone at this time accepted, and to one extent or another believed in, the magical universe whose physical form had been delineated centuries before by the Greek geographer Ptolemy, and which remained a constituent part of everyone's imagination regardless of Copernicus and the discoveries of later astronomers and explorers. It is simply that university-educated men developed a number of theories about witches and evil spirits, which gradually began to impinge upon everyone else's perceptions via the courtroom, the pulpit, the pamphlet and the place of execution.

28

A parallel may be drawn with modern Western Christianity. Society as a whole pays at least lip-service to a biblically based version of it. Professional theologians, however, very often develop a set of explanations which can differ considerably from those accepted by members of local congregations, and indeed the two versions may be remarkably dissimilar even though they are grounded on the same premises. But modern theologians do not often air their academic interpretations to the public at large or seek to bend the man or women in the street to their specialised point of view. What makes the fifteenth century different was the active intention of theologians, assisted by legislatures and lawyers, to impose their version of witchcraft on the people, a task made easier by the control the learned could exercise by preaching, by printing in the vernacular and by the public theatre provided by trials and executions.

Heinrich Institoris

Several different strands of opinion regarding witches and malefi-cent magic, then, were being woven together during the fifteenth century. There are five which are significant:

(1) *Elements of heresy*, such as the worship of a demon (idolatry) and blasphemy, including parody of sacred rituals and the very presence of witches at their Sabbat;
(2) *Malefices*, including raising storms, destroying crops, causing diseases and killing by means of magic;
(3) *Criminal acts*, such as murder and infanticide. The distinction between these and malefices is obviously blurred, but destroy-ing crops by magical means, for example, may reasonably be distinguished from destroying crops by purely human agency;
(4) *Marvellous elements which might be open to doubt*, of which the nocturnal flight of witches to the Sabbat is the clearest example;
(5) *Sexual elements*, in this context principally those indiscriminate orgies which allegedly took place during the course of a Sab-bat, and magical interference with a man's sexual potency, aimed at the ruination of Christian marriage.

Writers on witchcraft tended to emphasise one or more of these points – we have seen, for example, that Nider drew attention to malefices and his personal doubts about the ability of witches to fly, whereas the author of *Errores Gazariorum* preferred to underline the elements of heresy – but in 1486 there appeared a witchcraft treatise which forcibly, even imperiously, drew its readers' attention to the sexual elements of witchcraft: the *Malleus Maleficarum* (The Hammer of Witches) by the Dominican inquisitor Heinrich Krämer, also known as 'Institoris', possibly assisted by another Dominican, Jakob Sprenger.

Underlying the entire structure of the *Malleus* are three beliefs: (a) witchcraft is real and it is heresy to maintain the opposite; (b) evil spirits incessantly interfere in human affairs; and (c) both witchcraft and demonic activity are permitted by God for his own purposes. This last is very important. The phrase 'with God's permission' is found everywhere throughout the *Malleus*, (as, indeed throughout every similar witchcraft treatise or encyclopaedia of the period), and it is taken for granted that whatever malefices witches may attempt to do, whether of their own volition or at the prompting of an evil spirit, can be done only because God allows the Devil to perpetrate evil by means of human agents in order to test the good or punish the wicked. Institoris points to six ways in which witches can harm humanity: (a) by perverting love from its proper course; (b) inspiring negative emotions such as hatred and jealousy; (c) interfering with the sexual act and childbirth; (d) causing disease; (e) killing humans and animals; and (f) depriving people of their reason – all done, it should be noted by women.

Now, many treatises before the *Malleus* had used the word *maleficiorum* in their titles. It is a masculine genitive plural and refers to 'workers of harmful magic', the assumption being that these would include both males and females, according to Latin grammatical convention whereby a masculine noun or adjective may stand for both masculine and feminine references. Institoris, however, deliberately changes the word to its feminine form, *maleficiarum*, thus emphasising right from the start his perception, which he wishes to be absorbed and adopted by his readers, that witches are actually women rather than men. Strictly speaking, therefore, one should bring out this emphasis in any translation of the title: 'The Hammer of Females Who Work Harmful Magic'.

But why is it witches are women in particular? Because they are more credulous than men, says Institoris, and so more easily deceived by Satan; because they are more given to carnal lust than men, and Satan may use this not only to lead them astray but also to spread witchcraft itself through acts of venery; and because a woman is an imperfect animal and naturally a deceiver herself. The very word for woman in Latin, *femina*, he says, derives from *fe* and *minus*, 'a lesser thing in faith'. There was nothing new in this type of misogyny, of course. It had existed in the ancient world which provided many of the key texts commonly used to justify it [18; 39]. But Institoris brings an edge to the prejudice (so much so that his assertions often border upon farce, as can be seen from his ludicrous attempt at etymology), and the fact that the *Malleus* was specifically written to demonstrate to what he saw as an indifferent world what witches were really doing and how they could be stopped, and that the work went into at least eight editions before the end of the fifteenth century, makes us uncomfortably aware that his jaundiced emphases managed to receive a remarkable degree of publicity and acceptance. Nevertheless, this should not blind us to the fact that the *Malleus* is actually a very peculiar book and not altogether typical of witchcraft literature, although it is often referred to and quoted as though it were.

It is worth noting, too, that the work begins with an implicit lie. Institoris was careful to attach to his text a copy of a Bull by Innocent VIII, *Summis desiderantes*, issued by the Pope in December 1484 to give both Institoris and Sprenger the authority they needed to pursue their work as inquisitors in southern Germany. By prefacing the *Malleus* with this Bull, Institoris deliberately tried to create in his readers the impression that Innocent approved of the book and was giving it his official approval.

The fact is, however, Institoris was smarting from a serious reversal in his career. For during the summer of 1485, on the strength of that Bull, he had initiated investigations of witchcraft involving more than fifty people, all but two of whom were women, in the area round Innsbruck. By the beginning of October he was prepared to bring formal charges against seven of them, but the subsequent trial turned into a political battle between him and the Bishop of Brixen, George Golser, who was disturbed by the ferocity with which Institoris pursued the accused, and the illegal methods he was prepared to use to achieve convictions. The result was that Institoris was unsuccessful and the women were conditionally released [147]. Institoris's reaction was to write the *Malleus*, incorporating into it many of the initial depositions from the Innsbruck trial, in order to convince the relevant authorities that in future neither he nor other inquisitors should be hampered by legal niceties in the pursuit of witches; for the heretical-demonic threat posed to both Church and state by witches was so grave that their vigorous and unremitting persecution had become nothing less than imperative. We see, then, that the 'Hammer' of the title is none other than Institoris himself [**23**, *31–49*; **129**].

Ulrich Molitor

Now, the political figure most concerned in the Innsbruck trial was Archduke Sigismund of Austria. Some of the people questioned actually came from his household, and the Archduke has some-times been credited with encouraging not only the Innsbruck trial in 1485 but also another in Ravensburg the previous year. In fact, however, he seems to have held himself aloof from both proceed-ings, unwilling to become involved in a tussle between inquisitorial, episcopal and Papal claims to authority, and his apparent ambival-ence towards witchcraft itself can be seen in Ulrich Molitor's little treatise of 1489, *De Lamiis et Phitonicis Mulieribus* (Witches and Women Who Foretell the Future). This is cast in the form of a dialogue between Molitor, Conrad Sturtzel, the Archduke's sec-retary, and Archduke Sigismund himself. Sigismund's role in the dialogue is to ask questions of the two lawyers and to ex-press reservations about certain aspects of witchcraft, not all of which, one may note, are dismissed by the subsequent answers. The questions, which deal with many of the contemporary obsessions about witchcraft, are as follows.

(1)   Can witches, with the aid of an evil spirit, produce hailstorms, frosts and rain with a view to damaging the land?
(2)   Can they, with like aid, hurt adults and children by making them ill?
(3)   Can they cause impotence in men?
(4)   Can they change shape? (This is a question repeated later in a somewhat different form).
(5)   Can they fly on a stick or an animal to their Sabbat where they eat and drink and indulge in sexual orgies? (This question, too, is repeated).
(6)   Can the Devil have sex with women? (Repeated).
(7)   Can children be born of such a union?

(8) Can witches, with the help of an evil spirit, discover secrets, including the secrets of Princes, and can they predict the future?

(9) Can evil spirits affect the elements and human beings?

The kernel of the discussion is therefore the powers attributed to witches or the Devil, and the conclusion reached by the discutants is, on the whole, a negative one. The Devil cannot raise storms, nor can he cause others to do so. He cannot make men impotent unless God gives him the requisite permission so that the individual may be punished for his sins or have his fidelity tested, like Job, with a view to increasing his virtue should he survive the ordeal. Witches do not actually fly to their Sabbats. They merely think they do because they are subject to illusions produced by the Devil. Likewise, they do not really change shape except in their imagination which has been manipulated by the Devil to create such an effect. The Devil cannot generate children, although witches may sometimes unite sexually with an evil spirit in the form of an incubus. Nor can the Devil or witch foretell the future, since only God has true foreknowledge of events. But because the Devil may be alert to the signs, let us say, of an oncoming storm, he may let his witches know that it is coming and so create in them the illusion that they themselves have been able to predict or conjure it. Finally, witches can accomplish no malefice except with the aid of the Devil or one of his evil spirits.

The question of the exact nature and activity of an *incubus* (a male demon who has sexual intercourse with a human female) or a *succubus* (a female demon who has sexual intercourse with a human male), was one which exercised both theologians and physicians throughout the whole period of the witchcraft crisis. Is it possible, it ran, for spirits which are, by definition, non-corporeal to perform physical acts and carry and transmit corporeal substances which will end in the generation of a child? One of the exchanges between Sigismund and Ulrich illustrates the nature of this debate.

Sigismund: Do certain people claim that the Devil, in the guise of a succubus, can have sexual intercourse with a man, receive his semen and then, in the form of an incubus, spill it into a woman's womb and thus make her pregnant?

Ulrich: In my opinion, this cannot happen; for even if the semen could be collected and transmitted in such a way, it would not have the power to engender a child. In chapter 25, the Conciliator says, 'You should know that, according to Galen, this member (i.e. the testicles) is not the source of the power of generation even though the generative faculty exists within it. The reason is that it cannot accomplish its work unless an afflatus is emitted by the heart, which will regulate both the quantity and the quality of the semen'.... In consequence, this theory suggests to me that since the Devil is unable to make use of this afflatus which originates in the heart, or of its generative power, it is obvious that although he may receive the semen the moment it is emitted and transmit it to a woman, in the absence of the necessary attendant circumstances he will in no way be able to engender a child.

One must be careful, however, not to misunderstand these negative conclusions. Molitor is not denying the existence of Satan, evil spirits, witches or magicians. Nor does he deny that Satan can, under certain circumstances, perform extraordinary and wonderful acts. But he does say that Satan's power is limited by the two considerations we noted earlier: Satan cannot exercise the power he has except by permission of God, and his power is limited by the divine laws of creation, since the Devil himself, like humanity, is merely a creature – although because the Devil is an angel (albeit an evil one), he has a greater knowledge of the hidden workings of nature than that which is available to human beings and can therefore impose upon humans by reason of that greater knowledge. In effect, however, he deludes them by creating illusions which will mislead them into thinking they possess abilities they do not actually have, or at the very least into imagining they have access to and command over powers superior to their own. But Satan cannot have ultimate victory over human beings unless they deliberately and actively bind themselves to him by substituting him for God. Thus Molitor comes to the conclusion that witchcraft is essentially apostasy and idolatry, and for that reason witches should be put to death by the civil authorities. He ends his treatise, however, on a note of optimism. Satan is easy to overcome. All we need do is make the sign of the cross and his ability to exercise any power over us is rendered null at once.

One of the most distinctive features of Molitor's treatise is the series of woodcuts which illustrate the text (see **Figures 1–7**). These pictures are notable because *De Lamiis* is the earliest book on

Figure 1 A lawyer, perhaps Molitor himself, instructs everyone else, including the Church, in the ways of witchcraft.

Figure 2   A witch shoots a man in the foot to make him lame. The arrow has nine barbs so that the pain will be recurrent, or perhaps so that it will be more intense. It is possible that 'foot' is a synonym for 'penis', as it certainly is in ancient literature, in which case the picture would be illustrating magical interference with the sexual act.

witchcraft to be illustrated in this way and these pictures, crude though they may be, helped set the tone for subsequent illustrations in future works.

It is interesting to note which aspects of witchcraft Molitor has chosen to illustrate. Of the six pictures which deal directly with witches, two show an act of malefice; two show preternatural modes of travel to the Sabbat along with shape-changing of the witch or of the evil spirit; one shows witches at the Sabbat itself; and one a woman being seduced by Satan. Each stands for one or more of the questions asked by Sigismund and answered by Molitor.

The only subject he omits is divination of the future, and this is perhaps because divination was not a magical activity perceived as being peculiar to witches.

Figure 3 This illustrates two of Sigismund's questions: can the Devil change people's shapes, and can witches fly to the Sabbat on a stick or a wolf? Here three mutated witches are launched into flight on a long forked stick.

Figure 4 This shows a peasant on the back of a wolf-like creature. This refers to an incident described by Conrad Sturtzel, one of the participants in the dialogue, apropos witches going to the Sabbat. It happened, he says, not all that long ago while he was assisting at a court case in Constanz. According to the plaintiff, a peasant had appeared in front of him, quite without warning, riding upon a wolf, and this sight had been so unnerving that he had lost the use of his limbs. So he asked the peasant to remove the paralysis and the peasant (now referred to as 'the magician') agreed to do so provided the plaintiff promised not to talk about the incident. Since both men had ended in court, the plaintiff had clearly not kept his part of the bargain. It is a slightly curious anecdote, as it has no immediate connection with witches and the Sabbat; but the intended inference is likely to be that the peasant was in fact a male witch travelling to one of these diabolical conventions.

Among writers on witchcraft, Molitor is largely in the tradition of the *Canon Episcopi* and seems to be largely untouched by the singular preoccupations of the *Malleus Maleficarum*. There is, however, at least one sign that the *Malleus* may have had an effect, for Molitor tends to assume that witches will be women, and it is women in general he addresses near the end of his treatise: 'Women, remember the contract you made at your baptism and when you are

Figure 5 The Devil in the form of a man seducing a woman. The presence of a tail and the hand and foot of a bird of prey indicates to the viewer the real nature of her seducer, but there is no need for us to take these helpful signs literally. Written accounts, such as we find in indictments of accused witches, of meetings between a woman and the Devil, almost always give the impression that Satan appeared to her without any animal attributes (cloven feet, horns and the like), and that her seduction could easily have been mistaken for the successful advances of a lecherous human stranger.

tempted by the Devil, be strong and resist his suggestions; and for that purpose arm yourselves with the sign of the cross.' But apart from this, Molitor looks back to an earlier tradition of the Church, one which preoccupies itself more with heresy than with sex, and the importance of his contribution to witchcraft literature consists largely of his insistence on the presence and activity of the Devil in this world. For where Nider, the *Errores Gazariorum*, Tholosan, Martin le Franc and Institoris make great play of recording vivid, salacious details of what witches do, especially at their Sabbats, Molitor constantly draws his readers' attention to the figure of Satan and the limitations of diabolical power; and where Institoris emphasises the omnipresence of witches and the devastation they

Figure 6 Two female witches conjure a storm by throwing a cock and a serpent into a pot of boiling liquid. Raising storms by magic seems to have been one of the activities attributed to witches, particularly in the German states and the North.

Figure 7 Three female witches feasting at a Sabbat where, Molitor informs his readers, witches were accustomed to eat and drink before surrendering themselves to indiscriminate sexual pleasure. Little of this is evident in the picture. Indeed, it shows a remarkably demure ensemble, and one is reminded more of ladies taking tea in a living-room than of handmaidens to the Devil preparing themselves for an orgy.

are able to inflict on their own communities, Molitor reminds us that God, not Satan, is in charge of the world and that the Devil is easy to defeat because his power is limited and his abilities boil down to little more than the power to create illusion.

Concluding Remarks

Witchcraft, as generally interpreted at this time, seems to have acquired a Janus-like status, one face looking back towards a popular magic which was concerned largely with effecting cures, manipulating love or inflicting malefices upon people, crops or animals; the other peering into a future wherein the more sensational claims about witches became commonplace among those in authority and filtered through to the rest of society – the witches' flight, shape-changing, idolatry and apostasy at the Sabbat, wild sexual orgies ignorant of order or decency.

The *Malleus* seeks to validate the latter, adding to its descriptions of witches and recommendations to judges a deeply felt misogyny which may have owed as much to the personal animus of Institoris himself as to any prevailing theory about the quality and status of women. Molitor, on the other hand, maintains a certain distance from the sensationalism, stressing a point which Institoris seems almost in danger of forgetting, and one which would later be underlined by most Protestant writers on the subject – that God, not Satan, is master of this world and that witches may be deluded rather than assisted by the Devil.

4

The Effects of the Early Reformation

Preliminary Remarks

With the advent of change – some of it fundamental – in the doctrine and organisation of Christianity brought about by dissenting theologians at the beginning of the sixteenth century, the tension within Europe, which had been sustained throughout the previous hundred years, was racheted up still further. Political change, with its frequent accompaniment, war, became even more rapid; millennial fears increased; expectation of the imminence of the Apocalypse was as strong among Protestants as it had been hitherto (and continued to be) among Catholics. To this mixture was now added the missionary zeal of dissident Christian communities, each taking a view on the meaning of the presence in this world of large and apparently increasing numbers of magicians and witches.

The Jesuit Martin Del Rio expressed a common, widespread fear, when he wrote: 'These days, as we are taught by both reason and experience, we have to do battle, not with the delusions of credulous old women or apparitions which the half-witted see in their dreams, but with actual evil spirits whose power and counsel is used by practitioners of magic'; and he went on to blame the spread of these activities upon the diaspora of heretics, 'because evil spirits are accustomed to deceive people and cause them to fall into error, just as beautiful prostitutes do'.

So battle-lines were indeed drawn as Catholic and Protestant writers reacted to one another and sought to use their various opinions about witchcraft as weapons in a theological struggle for supremacy. On the one hand, those who were influenced by the *Malleus* attributed a great deal of effective power to the Devil. This tended, though not universally, of course, to be the Catholic point of view. Protestants, on the other hand, emphasised the omnipotence

43

of God and therefore saw the actions of witches and evil spirits as deceptive illusions or as transitory effects which were part of God's general plan for humanity. Neither of these views was compatible with the other. Nevertheless, there were large areas of agreement between the warring theologies and one must not make the mistake of imagining that Protestants were more sceptical than Catholics about the effects and intentions of witches' actions. Sixteenth-century scepticism on this subject, as we shall see, is not quite the same as ours.

Despite the proliferation of religious dissenters during the sixteenth century, only two can be said to have extended their influence far and wide across Europe and to have gathered whole nations under their respective banners: the German, Martin Luther and the Frenchman, Jean Calvin. Both accepted that witches and witchcraft were real enough, although Calvin in particular, like so many Catholic theologians before him, expressed reservations about certain aspects of witchcraft theory. Luther expressed similar doubts but also developed a novel approach towards the problem of witches in society, a problem he linked to the nature, purpose and destiny of women.

Luther

The *Malleus* had identified women as witches, explaining that women are naturally inclined towards corruption; that because of their lack of intelligence they fall prey more easily than men to the temptations and seductions of Satan; and that women left to themselves are undisciplined and governed by uncontrollable lust. Hence 'it is not surprising that one finds more women tainted by the heresy of those who work harmful magic than men' (1. 6). The natural inference from all this is that women become witches because their nature drives them to it: they can scarcely help themselves.

Luther, however, took a rather different and, indeed, a somewhat harsher view. Instead of emphasising women's raging sexuality, he drew attention to their weakness of body and intellect. 'Who can list all the histrionic, ridiculous, trivial, superstitious things pertaining to this sex which is so eager to be seduced?' he wrote. 'Right from the start, from Eve, they have had an inborn inclination to be deceived and to be regarded as no more than a plaything' (*Decem*

Praecepta Wittenbergensi Praedicta Populo, 1518). Hence, they need to be brought under control and above all need a purpose in life; and that purpose, he maintained, was not far to seek. If they were to devote themselves to being good wives and mothers under their husbands' gentle (and he emphasised *gentle*) correction, their excesses would be restrained and their tendency to over-emotionalism brought into proper balance. This is pleasing to God and will protect them against the temptations laid before them by Satan. What is more, it is in accord with that inner moral power with which women are also endowed – a God-given inclination to behave virtuously which is coexistent with their weakness and foolishness. In other words, women *choose* to become witches in the face of their better natures.

But what happens if a woman is not willing to submit herself to this pious regime and virtuous destiny? The sinful tendency she has inherited from Eve will, in times of stress or doubt, turn her towards the Devil as a source of advice and guidance, and because she is essentially an irrational being, unable to bring logic to bear on her situation or exercise rational judgement thereupon, she will be seduced by the superficial attractions of diabolical magic which will seem to offer her solutions to her problems and provide answers to her queries.

Luther's solution to the problem of women's natural instability, therefore, was to propose that they marry, have children and so sublimate their uncontrollable sexuality into the vocation of being a dutiful Christian housewife and mother. In consequence, he offered them a choice, as it were (housewife or witch?), and in doing so differentiated himself from the theory of the *Malleus* whose contention is that women become witches because they find it extremely difficult to do otherwise [23, 58–67].

Just how novel this interpretation was can be gauged by comparing it with the message conveyed by the images of witches produced by Luther's contemporary, Hans Baldung Grien. A woodcut of 1510 and two drawings of 1514 depict groups of women, a mixture of old and young, preparing themselves to fly to a Sabbat. The pictures are full of symbols of lust and folly, suggesting at once the deluded silliness of the women, and their abandonment to the demands of sexual excitement. Two more drawings of 1514 and 1515 take this last even further and suggest a concupiscence bordering on pornographic obscenity. Baldung's intention in producing these images seems to have been a desire to ridicule the notion that the witches' flight might be real – and here he was at one not only with earlier scholarly doubt but also with another of his contemporaries, Johann Geiler von Kayserberg, whose collected sermons on witchcraft, *Die Emeis* (The Ant-Heap), were published in German in 1517 – and yet Baldung cannot prevent a genuine terror of the Devil from informing his every line and communicating itself to the viewer. His pictures, though satirical in intent, are no joke and their deep-seated misogyny is coupled with a real belief in the reality of the witches' ecstatic alliance with Satan [59].

So, in as far as Luther grants women some choice in the matter, and offers them an acceptable way of dealing with their problems and avoiding the dangers inherent in their weak minds and bodies, he is less fatalistic about women than Institoris. Nevertheless, his view is scarcely less misogynistic – it is notable, for example, that in his German translation of a key Biblical text, 'Thou shalt not suffer a witch to live' (Exodus 22:18), he substituted the specifically feminine *zauberinen* ('women who work magic') for the inclusive Latin *maleficos* ('people who work harmful magic') – and his call for witches to be executed was no less stringent than that of his more influential predecessor.

Calvin

Calvin placed heavy emphasis on God's omnipotence and therefore noted that Satan, although 'the prince of this world', had liberty to operate only in as far as God was willing to allow. 'By permission the Devil may indeede trouble the aire, and also do other thinges, after which maner God is saide to send tempestes and hailes. And by whom doeth he it? By the wicked angels' (*Sermon on Deuteronomy* (1555), chapter 18). Peculiarly open to diabolical influence, he suggests, is any activity which departs from the natural order, and in consequence anyone who strays therefrom by wanting to obtain power or knowledge beyond that which is dictated by nature and permitted by God will come within the purlieu of the Devil and his evil spirits; and should this happen, he or she will be subject to diabolical illusions. 'It is a kinde of Inchauntment, that is to say of divelish illusion, when a man shall be made to thinke that one is transformed into a wolfe, or that he sees the shape of a thing that hath no substance or trueth indeed' (ibid.). Calvin thus agreed with some earlier Catholic scholars that certain aspects of what was claimed for magic and witchcraft deserved a degree of scepticism.

Like many of his contemporary Protestant writers and their successors, however, he advanced the confessional view that Catholicism both in belief and practice was little more than simple witchcraft and therefore worthy of condemnation: 'In Poperie all are witches in their idolatries.... God cuppleth those two sins together' (*Sermon on Deuteronomy*, chapter 18). This development can be seen especially in what might be termed 'the battle of exorcists', when an individual supposedly occupied or possessed by an evil spirit was made the object of prayers ands rituals designed to expel the demon. Catholics and Protestants alike often used these occasions and the results stemming therefrom to claim that God had thereby borne witness to the truth of one particular confession and demonstrated the sterility or superstitiousness of the other. One incident of 1566, for example, known as 'the miracle of Laon', saw the expulsion of Beelzebub from the body of a young girl, Nicole Aubrey, in consequence of the efforts of her Catholic exorcists, and this was quickly claimed as a triumph for the virtue and truth of Catholicism. Indeed, it was said that a number of Protestants reconverted to the faith as a direct result of witnessing the miracle [107, 43–5].

But if Calvin had doubts about some aspects of witchcraft, he had none whatever about the power of the Devil whom he saw leading humanity into the sin of idolatry via the two conduits of Catholicism and witchcraft [62]. So it is not surprising that he agreed with Luther that witches, at any rate, along with cunning-folk and any other practitioners of magic, should be uprooted from society.

It is not for us to suffer either inchanters or witches among us. And if these be forbidden, we must understand therwithall that all other kinds of Wizardrie are deadly crimes before God. And if Judges and Magistrats do their duties, it is certain that they will no more beare with them than with murthers.
(*Sermon upon Deuteronomy*, chapter 18)

James VI of Scotland

King James's foray into witchcraft literature happened because he himself had been the object of a widespread conspiracy of witches to murder him in 1589–90. The conspirators had applied themselves to several ways of doing this: (1) wrecking the royal ship on its return journey in 1590 from Denmark whither James had gone to bring back his bride to Scotland; (2) concocting a magical poison which was to be placed above a door-lintel or upon a threshold in one of the palaces, so that James might be infected as he passed by; (3) obtaining a piece of the King's linen, such as a shirt or a handkerchief, by means of which maleficent magic could be set in train; and (4) creating a wax image of the King, which would then be set near a fire so that the likeness would melt and the King, via sympathetic magic, would be consumed by fever or some other wasting illness. The plot was discovered and large numbers of witches, many of them from fishing-villages or sea-ports along the east coast of Lothian were arrested. The fate of most is unknown. Some of the principals were certainly executed. Others, however, were later set at liberty.

Their combined testimonies, one or two of which were allegedly extracted by torture (although the main source for that is a tendentious pamphlet clearly printed as propaganda), not only described their magical preparations to murder the King, but also gave details of a grand Sabbat held in the kirk of North Berwick during the dead of night on All Hallows' Eve, 1589. Over a hundred witches, it was said, male as well as female, gathered in the kirkyard and danced to the noise of a Jew's harp before entering the kirk where they found the Devil standing in the pulpit surrounded by candles which burned with a blue flame. Satan called the roll, much like a schoolmaster in charge of a class, demanded an account of his followers' wrong-doing, and urged them to increase their efforts therein. Then graves were violated, one inside the kirk, the other in the kirkyard, and their corpses dismembered so that the fingers and toes of the dead could be used in magical operations [86].

Now, it is this incident which has given James VI his reputation as a fanatical hunter of witches, a reputation he certainly does not deserve because both before and after the flurry of 1590–1 he seems to have been somewhat sceptical of the more sensational claims made by and about witches; and indeed, what one might call his balanced opinions were very much like those of Calvin. But the magical treason-conspiracy gave him a bad fright, a fright which underlies his remarks to the jury which tried one of the accused, Barbara Napier, in 1591:

Witchcraft, which is a thing growen very common amongst us, I know it to be a most abhominable synne, and I have bene occupied these three quarters of this yere for the siftyng out of them that are guylty heerein. We are taught by the lawes both of God and men that this synne is most odious, and by Godes law punishable by death: by men's lawe it is called *maleficium* or *veneficium*, an ill deede or a poysonable deede, and punishable likewise by death.

It was out of this experience, then, that he produced his short treatise on witchcraft, *Daemonologie*, published in 1597 but written earlier in *c*.1593. The book, cast in the form of a dialogue, is divided into three parts. In the first, James discusses magic in general and the part played therein by the Devil. Satan, he says, tempts people, both learned and unlearned, into magic by appealing to their curiosity. The learned he introduces to judicial astrology whereby they hope to see into the future, 'and so mounting from degree to degree upon the slipperie and uncertaine scale of curiositie, they are at last entised, that where lawfull artes or sciences failes, to satisfie their restles mindes, even to seeke to that black and unlawfull science of *Magie*' (1.3).

The unlearned he teaches how to make charms,

as commonlie daft wives uses, for healing of forspoken goodes, for preserving them from evill eyes, by knitting rowan-trees, or sundriest kinde of herbes, to the haire or tailes of the goodes: By curing the Worme, by stemming of blood, by healing of Horse-crookes, by turning of the riddle [a popular method of divination] or doing of such like innumerable thinges by wordes, without applying anie thing meete to the part offended, as Mediciners doe: Or else by staying married folkes to have naturallie adoe with other (by knitting so manie knottes upon a poynt at the time of their mariage), and such-like things... [and] unlearned men (being naturallie curious and lacking the true knowledge of God) findes these practises to proove true, as sundrie of them will doe, by the power of the Devill for deceaving men ... and being desirous to winne a reputation to themselves in such-like turnes, they either (if they be of the shamefaster sorte) seeke to bee learned by some that are experimented in that Arte (not knowing it to be evill at first) or else being of the grosser sorte, runnes directlie to the Devill for ambition or desire of gaine, and plainlie contractes with him thereupon. (1.4)

It is in Part 2 that James turns to witchcraft in particular, describing how Satan plays upon people's moral weaknesses to draw them into his service. 'Their mindes being prepared before hand . . . they easelie agreed unto that demande of his', namely, 'to renunce their God and *Baptisme* directlie'; whereupon he, 'gives them his marke upon some secreit place of their bodie, which remaines soare unhealed' (2.2). The Devil's mark, a point upon the body, which may be tested by inserting a long pin deep into the flesh without thereby causing any pain or bleeding, was a well-known feature of witchcraft theory, accepted by many as a sure indication of a person's being a witch. Professional witch-prickers, such as John Kincaid in Scotland and Matthew Hopkins in England, took advantage of this belief to set themselves up as experts on the subject and gain both money and prestige from their self-appointed function until circumstances revealed that each man was, in fact, a fraud. Curiously enough, the Devil's mark was rarely discovered in 'secret places' (i.e., the pudenda) during searches in Scotland. There it appeared almost always on the arm, the shoulder or the neck and, less frequently, on the side or leg.

Again James emphasises how Satan deceives the witch, and it is noticeable that he expends a deal of space on showing that witches' flights are no more than diabolical illusions. Women, he says, are more given to witchcraft than men because they are the frailer sex; and it is by God's permission that people are subject to Satan's temptations, either to punish them for their sins, stir up a faith grown sluggish, or test that faith for its strength, as Job was tested (2.5). No Catholic writer on the subject disagreed with him on either of these last two points.

Part 3 deals with ghosts and spirits, some of which may obsess or possess an individual, some of which are *incubi* and *succubi*. James, however, dismisses accounts of monstrous births stemming from sexual congress between witches and these spirits as no more than silly stories; but when it comes to the business of exorcism, he makes an interesting judgement. The proper, apostolic way to cast out devils, he says, is 'by the vertue of fasting and prayer, and incalling of the name of God', in other words, the methods used by Protestants. Catholics, however, 'though erring in sundrie points of Religion to accomplish this, if they use the right forme prescribed by CHRIST herein', may also exorcise successfully (3.4) – either a back-handed concession to religious opponents, or a dry way of suggesting that if Catholics were to convert, they would find themselves able to perform indeed what they could now merely claim to do.

From the *Daemonologie*, then, we gather (among much else, of course) that James was uncertain whether the witches' flight was real or not, but that he considered the Sabbat an indisputable fact. His uncertainty about the former was standard Protestant reaction, but in James's case his attitude to the latter may stem from his experience of listening to the East Lothian witches' evidence rather than from literary sources. For on the one hand, many of them told him they went to the Sabbat at North Berwick in riddles upon the sea (which could have been true if one substitutes the word 'coracles' for 'riddles'), while one of the principals, Agnes Sampson, said she was taken there on horseback by her son-in-law. No one mentioned broomsticks or shape-changing or demonic assistance. Whereas, on the other hand, they all confessed they had been present at North Berwick, and their accounts contained nothing overly sensational – no killing of children or sexual orgies, even though the Devil, they said, was present and everyone paid homage by kissing his buttocks. If, then, one reads James's book as a personal document, rather than as the unoriginal, almost perfunctory contribution to the witchcraft debate it has often been described, it springs into vivid life: the conversation of a monarch, who had just had a dreadful experience, with his people, very many of whom will themselves have suffered the maleficent attention of witches and who will therefore be interested in and benefit from his account.

Concluding Remarks

Many Protestant writers on witchcraft tended to be dubious about aspects of the prevalent official theory which described flight to and attendance at the Sabbat. This may be due in part to intellectual hesitations they shared with a number of pre-Reformation Catholics, a tradition of doubt which transcended confessional strife. But it may also owe something to that very strife, for if post-Reformation Catholic demonologists laid stress upon the reality of the flight and the horrors of the Sabbat, were not their Protestant opponents almost duty bound to demur and suggest the very opposite?

Nevertheless, this did not mean they rejected the basic notion that magical operations (of which the acts of witches were simply maleficent examples) could appear both real and effective to those who worked and suffered them. Luther, for example, was quite clear that storms could be caused by witches (*Lecture on Genesis*, 1541, 25.11) and that witches ('the Devil's whores') were rightly burned at the stake because they allied themselves with Satan in his fight against God (*On the Councils and the Church*, 1539).

> Through his witches he is able to do harm to children, give them heart trouble, blind them, steal them, or even take away a child altogether and put himself in the cradle in place of the stolen child. I have heard there was just such a boy in Saxony. He was suckled by five women and still could not be satisfied.
>
> (*Lecture on Galatians*, 1535, 3.1)

Yet these operations and their effects were in fact illusory, created by Satan to mislead people into sin:

> Witchcraft is nothing but an artifice and illusion of the Devil, whether he cripples a part of the body or touches the body or takes it away altogether. He can do this remarkably well, even in the case of old people. No wonder, then, that he bewitches children this way.... They say he is able to heal what he has crippled with his tricks. But he heals by restoring an eye or some other injured part of the body – not that it had really been injured; but the senses of those whom he bewitched, as well as of others who looked at the bewitched person, were so deluded that they did not regard it as an illusion but supposed it was a genuine injury.   (ibid.)

Both Luther and Calvin directed some of their condemnation of witches against the Catholic Church whose rituals, especially those of exorcism, they described as magical in form and idolatrous in intent.

> At times the Devil takes possession of a person and then lets himself be cast out by adjuration, blessing, etc. All this he does for the purpose of confirming his lies and deceptions and to impress the people, so that because of these apparently great miracles they are seduced into idolatry. (*Lecture on John*, 14.11)

Polemic, therefore, constituted a part of their intention when writing about any manifestation of magic [141]. But the essential

Protestant position was that in view of God's omnipotence the power of Satan must be limited, and that the Devil's efforts to dazzle the weak-minded (of whom women constituted the greater part) by means of theatrical illusions both could and should be resisted by strenuous personal effort – steadfast faith in God and constant prayer. The Church, said Protestants, had no counter-magic of its own to help. In that sense, in the battle against Satan, each person was on his or her own.

5

A Widespread Intent to Prosecute

Preliminary Remarks

The theory of witchcraft, then, was firmly in place by the time intense bursts of prosecution of witches broke out in various places in Western Europe late in the sixteenth century. Witches formed a sect of Devil-worshippers, mainly women since women were easily imposed on and driven by a sexual lust they found very difficult to control, and these made a pact either with Satan or with some other evil spirit, in return for which they were enabled by their demonic partner to exercise certain preternatural powers. These they employed for their own gain or, more usually, with vengeful and maleficent intent to cause loss and distress to the communities in which they lived. Their powers they could also use for apparent benefit – to cure illness, attract love or discover lost objects or treasure – but the benefits were illusory, indeed dangerous, for the recipient might thereby be led into losing his or her fear of Satan and, seduced ever further by illegitimate curiosity, steer perilously close to the weakness of faith on the one hand, and apostasy on the other.

Witches were examined in the extent of their wrong-doing by Satan who summoned them to Sabbats whither they flew through the air on sticks or animals, and at which they rendered an account of themselves, feasted, fornicated, received certain instruments of *maleficium*, such as variously coloured powders, and garnered ingredients for their magical ointments by killing young children, boiling down their bodies and skimming off the fat.

The number of witches was on the increase, for the Apocalypse was near and Antichrist would soon make his appearance. (Indeed, it was a Protestant commonplace that he had already arrived in the form of the current Pope.) Soon the last battle between God and the

Devil, newly loosed from his thousand-year captivity, would be joined and it was the duty of the Church and the civil magistracy to unite in extirpating the evil's human troops. The rapid increase in the number of heretics, wrote post-Reformation Catholic demonologists, made the spread of magic easier, for witches and heretics went together; and where magic and heresy were to be found, there also was Satan.

But if this was the theory which fuelled the prosecution, what actually happened in real life? A number of important points need to be made before we try to answer that question.

(1) The period of concentrated pursuit of witches in Western Europe was quite short, *c.*1580–*c.*1660, with a more intensive period beginning in 1590 and ending in *c.*1630.

(2) These intense outbursts happened for different reasons. Sometimes they coincided with a time of crisis in the countryside, as in the south of Germany during the 1580s and 1590s, where they were interpreted as portents of God's anger. But, as Behringer has warned (referring to Germany), 'while we can formulate a rule that witch hunts mostly began in years of agrarian crisis, we cannot infer the converse that they were the inevitable consequence of them' [15, 97; 14]; and indeed Scotland provides an example of a region in which there does not seem to have been any correlation between natural disasters and the prosecution of witches [73, 204–5].

(3) Witchcraft was not the monolithic system suggested by official witchcraft theory. Indeed, when one looks even at a cross-section of the thousands of indictments brought against alleged witches, it rapidly becomes clear that a very large number of charges relate to acts of magic which have little or nothing to do with the sensational aspects of the witch-theory. They deal with curing, with love-magic, and with malefices directed against individuals for whom the witch entertained ill-will. Often it is the case that Satan does not come into the picture, save by the silent implication that there must have existed some kind of pact between the witch and him. In Scotland, for example, the Devil is scarcely mentioned during the witch-trials of the sixteenth century (1590–1 excepted for reasons peculiar to the treason-trials of those years), whereas he begins to make regular appearances in indictments during the trials of the late 1650s and early

1660s. The thrust of prosecution, therefore, also differs from region to region and from period to period and regional studies are beginning to illustrate very clearly that no single or over-arching explanation for outbursts of witch prosecution is satisfactory [24].

(4) Likewise, suggested numbers of those executed for witchcraft are highly speculative, for there are so many variables. How many witches were arrested, and of these how many were found guilty and put to death? How many died in prison awaiting trials? How many committed suicide while they were in prison, or succumbed to the hardships and insanitary conditions of confinement? How many were lynched? How many of those arrested were found innocent and set free – a point frequently overlooked? Projected numbers of executions range from 40,000 (regarded by a majority of witchcraft scholars as a credible estimate) to a million (undoubtedly much exaggerated), but until the archives of Europe have been more thoroughly explored and their contents examined and assessed – a task increasingly undertaken by the new generation of historians of the subject – any suggested figure will stand in need of constant revision.

Uprooting Satan's Troops

Providing a list of places in which prosecution of witches was particularly intense during the decades c.1580–c.1630 has been done many times and there is little point in repeating the exercise [125, 19–24; 99, 55, 75–7]. From the evidence available, it is clear that the worst examples often owed much to the presence of a single individual who acted as a catalyst for local emotions which had been raised to boiling point by a variety of different factors.

In Trier, for example, during the reign of Archbishop Johann VII von Schönenberg (1581–99), twenty-two villages found themselves at the heart of persecution and, by the time the crisis was passed, two of those same villages were left with only two inhabitants, the rest having been executed [119]. The Archbishop, however, did not at first rush to the prosecution of witches and his later enthusiasm is likely to have been stimulated by his suffragan bishop, Peter Binsfeld (1540–98), whose book *Tractatus de Confessionibus Maleficorum et Sagarum* (Treatise on the Confession of Workers of Harmful Magic and Witches), published in 1589, replaced the *Malleus* in Germany as the foremost guide to recognising and dealing with witches. While professing a degree of moderation in his attitude to magic and witchcraft, Binsfeld in fact promoted a very stern line indeed. Witches, he said, profaned the sacraments, hated their native country and conspired together to ruin vineyards and harvests and thus cause widespread famine; and since the 1570s and 1580s saw crop failures in many parts of Germany, and since climate change produced long, cold winters and cold, wet summers which affected the vineyards round Trier, it is not surprising that his remarks seemed to be confirmed by local experience and thus carry a weight of truth.

Magistrates, he went on, who did not actively prosecute witches were failing in their duty and deserved to feel God's anger, and they should not hesitate to employ torture to extract the evidence needed for a conviction. His reason for this was simple. One can avoid using torture only if one has witnesses who are able to prove the charges laid against the accused, and such witnesses are actually never available because witches perform their evil deeds under cover of darkness, and what individual who takes his or her religion seriously would ever be present at a gathering of witches? Respectable (and therefore trustworthy) people are in their beds during the hours of night. Thus, 'because of the peculiar difficulty of obtaining proof with respect to clandestine deeds which are carried out in secret, guesswork and inference, which in other cases would not be adequate, are sufficient to act as proofs in this'; and on the strength of this type of initial denunciation, it was permissible to arrest someone and proceed to torture to obtain a confession.

It is the argument (not peculiar to Binsfeld) that because witchcraft has features which are not to be found in any other crime, it should be treated as a *crimen exceptum*, a crime to which the normal rules of evidence and proof need not be applied. Christina Larner has provided an apt comment on this situation.

The crime of witchcraft went on the statute books, or became otherwise the responsibility of secular powers, at a time when jurisdictions were becoming more centralised and more rationalised and when standards of proof were becoming rather closer to those of our own day. . . . The management of trials for witchcraft apparently ran counter to much of this emerging rationalisation and depersonalisation of criminal law and practice. [**73**, *87*]

Other Catholic German dioceses show a similar pattern. Julius Echter von Mespelbrunn, Bishop of Wurzburg (1573–1617), Johann von Bicken, Archbishop of Mainz (1601–4), Ferdinand of Bavaria, Archbishop of Cologne (1612–37), Johann Christoph von Wetterstetten, Bishop of Eichstätt (1612–36), Johann Gottfried von Aschhausen, Bishop of Bamburg (1610–22) and his successor Philipp Adolf von Ehrenberg (1623–31), and Georg Friedrich Greiffenklan von Vollrads, Bishop of Mainz (1626–9), all directed significant waves of prosecution of witches. Their motives were of the highest, for all were preoccupied with the menace presented to their flocks by what appeared to be the ever-increasing advance of Satan, whether he was to be seen in heretics or other deviants from desirable social, political or religious norms, and many, such as Ferdinand of Bavaria, were personally devout and therefore saw the prosecutions as a necessary surgery upon the body politic.

Likewise, between 1576 and 1635, Lorraine, which was much concerned with the advance of Protestantism along its frontiers, witnessed large numbers of witches brought before a number of judges distinguished by their severity, of whom the best known is Nicolas Rémy. Rémy was an advocate and thus had plenty of opportunity both to observe and take part in witch-trials, and it was out of this experience that he produced the somewhat chaotic mélange of personal reminiscence, anecdote, court-record and quotation which form his book *Daemonolatreia* (Worshipping an Evil Spirit as though he were God), in the preface to which he makes the claim that he had condemned to death as many as 900 witches in the decade between 1581 and 1591: and although one may need to make allowances for exaggeration, the number is not altogether impossible.

Rémy had a comforting and not unusual view of the immunity granted magistrates by God against the magical power of an arrested witch. 'You judges are fortunate that we can do nothing against you', he was told by one, while another admitted she had tried to revenge herself magically upon the magistrate who had had her arrested and tortured: 'I freely confess that all my endeavours are of no avail because [magistrates] are under God's special care and protection, and only God can counteract my plans.'

But it was not only Catholic countries which saw influential individuals directing large-scale prosecutions, or at least bearing a major responsibility for their outbreak and continuation. We have already noted that James VI of Scotland took an active personal interest in the magical treason conspiracy of 1590–1, although his role as persecutor has been much exaggerated. Similarly, his contemporary, Christian IV of Sweden, took fright at certain witchcraft events of 1612–13 and his nervousness, allied to the presence of a particularly strict Lutheran theologian in the relevant diocese, provides a parallel with the temporary preoccupation of James VI with crimes of witchcraft [63]. In the east of England between 1645 and 1646, two professional witch-finders, Matthew Hopkins and John Stearne, claimed to recognise (largely by pricking the accused to see if they could find an insensitive spot known as 'the Devil's mark') a large number of witches, many of whom were subsequently executed; and in Fife and East Lothian, the Scottish witch-finder John Kincaid performed a similar office with similar consequences.

Personal influence, however, could work in the opposite direction. At Logrono in Navarre, an *auto-da-fé* held during the autumn of 1610 initiated wholesale prosecution of witches among the Basques, whose confessions produced alarm in both ecclesiastical and secular authorities, for it seemed the accused were admitting to activities which covered the spectrum of those alleged by learned witchcraft theory – worshipping the Devil at Sabbats, concocting flying ointments and so forth. Naturally these allegations attracted the attention of the Spanish Inquisition, which sent several of its members to investigate. These included Alonso de Salazar Frias, who had been one of those appointed to deal with the *auto-da-fé* at Logrono and had not been satisfied even then with the quality and credibility of the evidence emanating from the witches' interrogations. From May 1611 until the end of the year, he talked to nearly two thousand witches who were willing to speak openly and truthfully to him because the Inquisition had agreed in March to an amnesty for witches, which allowed them to confess their crimes without fear of retribution. Salazar's questioning was thorough. He subjected priests to rigorous quizzing, spoke to witnesses separately so that he could compare their stories, and conducted experiments on animals to test what the witches claimed for their powders and ointments; and a reading of his account makes it quite clear that a person of the period was quite capable of believing in the reality of magic, witchcraft and witches while at the same time retaining the capacity to exercise independence of judgement and straightforward common sense.

His immense report (5,000 pages) came to the conclusion that the whole dreadful episode had been sparked by the enthusiasm of one inquisitor intent on sniffing out witches, and that the evidence he himself had heard and recorded was not sufficient to prove a single instance of genuine witchcraft. Despite disagreement from the other inquisitors who had been appointed along with him, Salazar's report was accepted by the Inquisition which, in 1614, in accordance with what he had suggested in his report, issued instructions for the guidance of inquisitors who had to deal with witches. These instructions

> insisted on external evidence to confirm the accusations made by accused witches; witches could retract their confessions without fear of torture; confessions were to be thoroughly investigated, but there was to be no confiscation of property in a matter of such doubt. No action was to be taken in any tribunal of the Spanish Inquisition without a unanimous vote, and all such actions involving witchcraft were to be forwarded to the Suprema [the highest council of the Inquisition] for review.   [**115**, *429*]

All pending cases of witchcraft were then dropped, and the property of those executed at Logrono in 1610 was returned to their families. It was, in fact, the end of all trials for witchcraft in Spain save for a small number which appear in later records from time to time [**58**, *387–9*].

Motives for Prosecution

It is important to realise that both individual prosecutions and those persecutory waves often designated 'hunts' were stimulated by a variety of motives, not just one. Personal religious enthusiasm bordering on fanaticism we have already seen in some of the German bishops. Monetary gain, too, could certainly play a part, for executing a witch was very expensive – the fuels for burning were not cheap, and there were the wages of various officials to be paid, not least those of the executioner himself – and so any goods or property the convicted witch might have was commonly forfeit to the state. But sometimes the whole, or a portion of the whole, might be awarded to the persons who had discovered the witch in the first place, an open invitation in the absence of legislation to the contrary to corruption and personal animus.

Climate change starting in the 1560s; economic difficulties brought about by crop failures and the effects of war; religious divagation leading to increased and rigorous disciplining of people by both ecclesiastical and secular authorities to enforce acceptance and strict observation of reformed religion, whether Catholic or Protestant; widespread belief that the world was entering its final phase and that the last battle with Satan was joined or about to be joined – all these produced a general climate of anxiety in which prosecution of anyone deemed to be a cause or a possible cause of increasing that anxiety was likely to be triggered.

Anabaptists provide a good example, for in the Netherlands a marked increase in prosecution of witches during the 1560s followed a sustained campaign to suppress Anabaptists during the 1540s and 1550s, a pattern which can be noticed in Germany as well. The reason for this seems to be that there was a certain conflation of perceptions in the popular mind which saw both magical practitioners and Anabaptists not only as disturbing deviants from the preferred social and religious norms, but also as agents of Satan forming demonic sects which posed a threat to true religion [140].

Sermons and pamphlets contributed to inflame this kind of situation. When a German news sheet of 1588, for example, informed its readers that 18,000 witches had recently met with the aim of devastating the countryside, it is not surprising that people felt threatened and took steps to protect themselves; and in consequence it made sense for the local population to demand redress and for responsible, conscientious rulers to accede to that insistence – a combination which produced both an increased brutality in the administration of criminal justice, and a rise in the number of executions for all kinds of offences, not merely witchcraft [77; 44, 45].

So, it would be foolish to try to offer a single explanation for the intensity of witch prosecution; and yet if there is indeed some kind of common thread (regardless of the official line on the need to preserve public order and ensure the salvation of souls), any study of the records reveals that it may consist of the motives for most of the prosecutions – variations upon struggles for power and status between members of small communities, who were constantly engaged in preserving their individual honour against the multifarious pinpricks of daily intercourse in the enclosed, almost hothouse atmosphere of village and parish, and who were also making a final attempt to allay personal fears grown too great for bearing [117, 257]. One should also make the point that in these localised tussles for status in which one party was deemed to possess the awful advantage of magical power while the other did not, the physical or economic weakness of either side would be largely irrelevant. In trials of strength, the stronger wins, and sometimes that gave victory to the witch, sometimes to the non-magical members of her or his community.

Women

It is still a common belief that witches were largely old, ugly, poor women living on the margins of their societies, that many if not most were widows, and that their childlessness was a cause of envy in themselves and fearful suspicion in others, especially perhaps in the case of English witches who were alleged to suckle familiars in a grotesque parody of normal wet-nursing culture [106, 244–60]. While there is much in this that may have been true of certain areas at certain periods, the English evidence should not be allowed to distort the picture, although it is used by Diane Purkiss to make the important point, applicable to most parts of Europe, that many acts of a witch's malefice involved precisely those cultural activities peculiar to or particularly associated with women, such as giving or attending birth, preparing food, attending to sickness, caring for the house, looking after farm animals – in general, exercising maternal and domestic authority – and hence it is to be expected that a majority of those denouncing women as witches would be women rather than men [111, 91–118].

Now, we have already seen that there were two streams of Classical precedent for the learned who wished to formulate a picture of the witch, (a) young and beautiful, and (b) old and ugly, both of which were employed by artists during the early modern period. If the second eventually turned out to be the more common, one should not really be surprised, since the witch was constantly presented in popular print, as well as in learned demonology, as the antithesis of desirable womanhood, and most of the iconography of the witch in sixteenth-century German art, for example, was derived from these written sources [36]. Moreover, there is plenty of evidence, of which Scotland provides one example, that the practice of magic, including witchcraft, spread much further up the social scale than the poor or beggarly. We must therefore beware taking literally every instance which seeks to portray the witch as old, ugly and marginalised. Such descriptions formed an essential part of the propaganda; they were not intended to provide readers or listeners with a likeness drawn from life.

One should also note that women were not accused of being witches because they were women. They were accused of being witches because the activities known as 'witchcraft' were closely associated with the kind of moral and physical weaknesses to which women were considered to be especially, but not exclusively, prey. One may perhaps draw a parallel with crimes involving physical violence. These are associated with men because the common cultural expectation is that men rather than women commit such crimes; and indeed our prisons are full of confirmatory evidences. But physical violence is not exclusive to men and if some women are found guilty of it, their conviction causes slight surprise (because it is relatively unusual) but not disbelief. If, then, the heart of witchcraft, as opposed to magical activity in general, lies in the practice of *maleficium*, it is clear that it is a form of magical operation which can be performed equally well by either sex, although the expectation of early modern Europe was that it would usually be performed by women [49; 31, 110]. Francis Bacon expressed much the same thought thus:

> The tying of the point upon the day of marriage, to make men impotent towards their wives, which . . . is so frequent in Zant and Gascony, if it be natural, must be referred to the imagination of him that tieth the point. I conceive it to have the less affinity with witchcraft, because not peculiar persons only, such as witches are, but any body may do it.   (*Sylva Sylvarum*, 1627, century 10)

Men

Witches, though largely female, also included men. Briggs suggests they constituted about one in four of those accused, although the proportion varied from place to place. Over half the 1,300 defendants whose cases came before the Parlement of Paris after 1565, for example, were men, while in Rouen the proportion was even higher – three out of every four [132; 95]. Men therefore turn up in court records in varying but significant numbers.

In Normandy there are one or two isolated cases before the apogee of witch-trials in the region, several of them involving shepherds accused of stealing Hosts for a male magician, or magically causing the deaths of people and animals over a period of twenty years. But then, between *c*.1585 and *c*.1615, came a flurry of prosecutions. A brief résumé of the male cases heard by the Parlement of Rouen in 1605 will give a good notion of the crimes of which they were accused (the details come from Monter).

March: *Shepherd aged 50.* He had refused to work magical cures for the relatives of a local official, and a toad was found among his possessions. He was hanged.

April: *Labourer.* He had tried to lift the bewitchment laid on some horses by another person. He had also quarrelled with the wife of a local official who then reported him to the ecclesiastical authorities. He was released.

Priest, notorious for fornication and for finding lost objects by divination with a mirror. He also kept a small collection of magical formulae for curing illnesses, and a list of magical characters and invocations of evil spirits. He was hanged.

May: *Shepherd aged 20.* He was accused of witchcraft and blasphemy and sentenced to the galleys for life.

Shepherd aged 50. He was accused of making a demonic pact and knowing how to protect his flock from wolves by means of a magical prayer. When they searched him, they found the Devil's mark on his left side. He was hanged.

June: *Shepherd.* He was accused of performing magic at a wedding with a view to causing impotence in the groom.

Apothecary. He was accused of trying magically to undo that impotence-magic, and of possessing a book of magic and papers containing invocations of evil spirits. He was sentenced to ten years in the galleys.

September: *Labourer aged between 35 and 40.* He was accused of learning witchcraft from his wife who was the principal defendant during this hearing. He was sentenced to life in the galleys.

Man (no job, no age given). He confessed that sick people used to come to him for advice on how their bewitchment could be cured or lifted. He was hanged.

Man aged 80. He was accused of being caught with a box containing toads and mysterious powders, and of having the Devil's mark on his right shoulder. He was hanged.

The fact that these defendants were men did not aid them in court. Undoubtedly the life sentences in the galleys were tantamount to a death sentence, and the ten-year sentence may have proved little better. Similarly, the five men who stood trial between December 1582 and March 1583 in Sancerrois, a hill region on the eastern border of Berry, were all executed: as was George de Haut in Lorraine, found guilty of witchcraft by Nicolas Rémy and sentenced by him to be burned alive on 4 May 1596.

Levack makes various suggestions in respect to male witches [78, 125]. (1) They may have been involved in treason. So they may, but the episode affecting James VI indicates that many more women than men were involved in that magical conspiracy, so treason cannot be seen as an especially male domain. (2) They may not actually have been witches, but rather sorcerers. We have seen earlier that it is more or less impossible to define 'witchcraft' and 'sorcery', at least in a Western context, so the distinction is difficult to see. It is true that men and not women were ritual or ceremonial magicians because this form of magic (sometimes referred to as 'high' magic as opposed to 'low' or 'popular') required an advanced level of literacy and at least a fair degree of competence in a number of different occult disciplines, and this level of knowledge was not available to most of the women who were likely to be accused of practising witchcraft. But then, neither was it available to most of the men who found themselves in that position, either. Male witches, as can be judged from the records, by and large operated the same magic for the same reasons and for the same purposes as female. (3) They may have been heretics, or suspected of heresy, in addition to their being magical practitioners. This is just as true of their womenfolk. (4) They may have been swept up as husbands, brothers, uncles, sons, in the growing whirl of a widespread series of witch prosecutions. This is perfectly true. The larger number of women accused of being witches meant that there was a greater opportunity of their male relatives' being accused as well. If, on the other hand, a man was the principal defendant, it was rare for his female relatives to be accused along with him.

Children

Children appeared in witch-trials as victims, as witnesses and as defendants. During the Mediaeval period they tended to be seen as victims, sacrificed to the Devil during a Sabbat, their bodies rendered to provide fat for flying-ointments or the constituents of those powders which witches scattered to cause sickness and death. The Jesuit demonologist Martin Del Rio addressed the theological problem presented by this slaughter of the innocents.

It is [the witches'] very frequent habit to do harm to very small children. God allows this, even in the case of those who have been baptised, because then they will be preserved from committing a good many sins and so be swept up into Heaven, free from danger, since wickedness will have no effect on their spiritual or mental faculties . . . and if they have not yet been baptised, God often allows them to be killed so that they may not suffer a worse fate on account of the sinful acts he has foreseen they would have committed had they lived. (*Disquisitiones Magicae*, 1599–1600, Book 3)

During the early modern period, the emphasis shifted and children were increasingly seen as vessels of demonic possession, thus playing a role as living rather than dead entities in the war with Satan. The Salem case of 1692 in North America is perhaps the best-known example of children claiming to be possessed as the result of malefice by adults whom they proceeded to name, but it is by no means unusual. Over a hundred years before, in 1589, the English village of Warboys saw a group of children from a wealthy, influential family terrorise a 76-year-old woman by accusing her of bewitching them. Protracted accusation, and the evident belief of other adults that the children were telling the truth, led to the old woman's confessing that she was indeed a witch; whereupon she was arrested, along with her daughter and husband, and all three were lodged in gaol. A trial followed, at which all three were found guilty and subsequently hanged [**128**, *79–82*].

The danger of taking seriously children's confessions and accusations is here made plain, although it would not be valid or prudent to draw the conclusion that children's evidence, no matter how sensational in content, is always unbelievable, and some such consideration clearly occurred to the judicial authorities of the sixteenth century, for they came to the conclusion that children could be important factors in solving a legal conundrum: since acts of witchcraft took place in secret, or at least unseen by anyone save the witch and perhaps his or her attendant evil spirit, how could it ever be possible to produce in court witnesses who would be able to give credible evidence against the accused? The answer, as Binsfeld pointed out in his treatise on witchcraft, lay in the concept *crimen exceptum*. If the standard rules did not apply, evidence could be obtained from witnesses not usually admitted as trustworthy – people hostile to the accused, those whose characters were suspect, known, convicted or suspect witches, the accused's accomplices, and children.

But once this solution was reached, the likely consequences followed as children accused adults of attending a Sabbat, or inflicting them with an evil spirit, or teaching them witchcraft and trying to make them servants of Satan. Opportunities for self-indulgence, whether intentionally malicious or not, were innumerable and the effect of children's confessions depended almost entirely on the care with which they were examined by an official. In the Warboys case, the results were tragic because the officials were careless and credulous. The Spanish inquisitor Alonso de Salazar Frias, on the other hand, confronted by a girl – one of 1,384 children accused of witchcraft, whom he questioned during his tour of duty in the Basque country in 1611 – who told him she was a witch and had had sexual intercourse with the Devil, an experience so violent that she nearly bled to death, had her examined by a group of women who quickly established that she was, in fact, a virgin. Salazar then gave the girl a stern warning about the possible consequences of her fantasising, and sent her home. Similarly, in 1683 a 13-year-old girl from Protestant Leonberg in Germany confessed to being a witch and said she had participated in more than one Sabbat, including in her story sensational details about riding a goat and being given poison wherewith to kill another child. More and more adults became involved, either as named participants in her tales about the Sabbats, or as parents whose children were threatened by her dangerous behaviour, or as officials who were called on to investigate her extraordinary and aggressive claims. Fortunately, the officials were cautious and did not allow the situation to get out of hand. Thus, there was no hysteria and no fatal consequence [122, 94–112]

Child witches, however, could be and often were punished severely. Indeed, many were executed. Henri Boguet, a French advocate who wrote one of the definitive legal textbooks on witchcraft, *Discours des sorciers* (1610), based upon his own judicial experience over a period of two years, declared that because witchcraft was such a dreadful crime, and because its practitioners rarely if ever reformed, children should not be immune from either torture or execution; and indeed Boguet followed his own advice and both tortured and executed pre-pubertal children. Nor were such things limited to Franche-Comté where Boguet was judicially active. Whole gangs of witch-children, mainly boys, were imprisoned or executed during the seventeenth century in Würzburg, Bamberg, Styria, Tyrol, Salzburg and Bavaria; while the Calvinist authorities in Guernsey during the same period were faced with trying to reform frightening assaults by young men upon young women during the Christmas period, a ritual activity known as 'werewolfery' which betrays links with shape-changing and 'the damnable art' (i.e., witchcraft) [101].

Walinski-Kiehl links some of this with a growing emphasis placed by adults on young people's capacity for sin, and therefore with those same adults' desire to impose stricter discipline on children with a view to reforming their morals. 'Children and adolescents', he says,

> who were involved in disreputable activities such as begging were also potential witch-suspects.... Some individuals also experimented with various forms of sorcery because of the potential power over nature that magic might give them. When these persons came before a court, often initially on theft or vagrancy charges, they also admitted to performing witchcraft practices. [142, *184*].

Hence they could be and indeed were perceived as offering a multiple moral and physical threat to the regular order of society and so were deserving of extirpation along with their adult counterparts.

Cunning Folk

One of the most noticeable features of witch-trial documents is the relative paucity of references to classic witch behaviour: transvection to the Sabbat and its attendant worship of the Devil, infanticide, feasting and orgy. These charges do appear, of course, and in large numbers; but far more common are accusations of curative or love-magic, *maleficia* against human beings, animals or crops, and the undoing of bewitchment cast by others. *Maleficia* apart, these read like acts of beneficent magic which were sought and, as in any other business transaction, usually paid for, by the witch's neighbours often over the course of one, two or even three decades before a sudden crisis turned first one and then several members of the community against her, and she found herself accused in front of a local official. In other words, the more common sort of witch's indictment prefers a number of charges which might be considered more typical of a cunning man or woman than of a witch. Why, then, were charges brought at all? Why was someone found guilty of witchcraft (as opposed to beneficent magic) under these circumstances? Are we to infer that the community could not or would not tell the difference between a cunning person and a witch, or that the law, whether ecclesiastical or secular, did not distinguish between the two and therefore treated all accusations of magic as though they involved the same type of offence [19]?

To some extent, the questions are formulated on a false premise: that the early modern period carefully distinguished between people offering a similar kind of service. But, as Katharine Park has pointed out, no such distinctions were made. Between 1393 and 1395, Francesco and Margherita Datini sought help for their continuing childlessness after several years of marriage. Margherita consulted a woman who offered to make her a poultice, a doctor who gave both diagnosis and medical advice, a member of the family who recommended a belt with a magical incantation inscribed on it, and her husband who said she should practise religious charity [105]. Here, then, we have very different solutions for a single problem, none regarded by any of the parties concerned as mutually exclusive. Margherita was able, in fact, to seek a wider range of assistance than most modern Western Europeans would consider appropriate, since for her there existed the possibility of magical and religious aid as well as medical and empirical. What is more, physicians themselves were perfectly prepared to offer magical healing along with their natural remedies, however they might hedge their advice with cautious reservation. So although people were well aware of the difference between, let us say, a doctor and a magical healer, in practice the recommendations or medicines offered by each might easily fall within the other's special province; and, likewise, a witch and a cunning person, both practitioners of magic, might seem to impinge on each other's particular field of expertise.

One says 'seem' because in this case perceptions were all-important. Our understanding of the relationship between witch and cunning person, however, is bedevilled by our uncertain grasp of the terminology used by the learned recorders of information relating to magic and witchcraft. It is often assumed that the theologians, demonologists, lawyers and doctors who wrote about these subjects made no lexical distinction between magicians, soothsayers, diviners and so forth because they regarded them all as either equally reprehensible or equally deluded; and that when it came to the actual practice of bringing these various practitioners into court, distinctions may well have been forgotten or discarded for the sake of higher ends, such as the elimination of anyone who might endanger society by trafficking with Satan.

Nevertheless, lexical differences do seem to have mattered. Take, for example, the observations of the English antiquary, William Camden, on what he calls the superstitions of the Irish.

> Should a cow become useless [i.e., dry], they send for a female practitioner of magic (*maga*), and she employs herbs whereby the cow falls in love with another cow's calf and in consequence starts to give milk again.
>
> They think a woman who asks for fire on May Day is a worker of harmful magic (*malefica*), and they will not give her any unless someone in her household is sick. Even then they give it with a curse because they think that next summer she will surreptitiously steal all their butter.   (*Britannia*, 1590)

Here there is a distinction between *maga* and *malefica*, in as much as the former is seen as a woman performing beneficent and the latter as a woman performing harmful magic, and Camden preserves these distinctions throughout his section on superstition. Unfortunately, we are not told whether the cases describe two women or one. Now, very often, cunning folk had a single skill – they could cure headaches but not skin disease, for example, or their magic was effective with animals but not with people – and so they were not consulted except when their particular gift or power was required. It is possible, therefore, that Camden's *maga* specialised in curing cows. On the other hand, her magical skills may have extended further and this instance happens to be the only one Camden has heard or read about; or the same woman may have turned her magical powers to good or evil ends, depending on what she was asked to do, in which case she may have been referred to as a *maga* on one occasion and a *malefica* on another.

Preservation of these lexical distinctions, then, implies that the learned were perfectly aware of the differences between 'cunning person' and 'witch' and that they used different terms (a) to describe different people or (b) to designate the same person employing magic for different ends on different occasions. In either case, however, but especially in the latter, it is clear that niceties were not always preserved when it came to prosecution, and the indictments of witches very often reveal that although most accusations against them relate to beneficent magic, there may be sufficient items relating to acts of harmful magic to warrant the accused's arrest and appearance in court. It is not that the authorities could not tell the difference between a cunning person and a witch; simply that magic is magic, and if someone is able to use it, she or he may use it for good or bad ends indiscriminately according to her client's request, and therefore a person's claim to employ beneficent magic is no defence since it is perfectly possible (and proved by so many examples from all over Europe) that she or he would be willing to turn that power to inflict either harm or death.

Both Catholic and Protestant writers vilified cunning folk on the grounds that their magical powers must depend on a pact with the Devil. Protestants, however, were especially fierce in their denunciations, perhaps because they tended to see many folk practices as remnants of Catholicism, which they decry as superstitious and mark down for eradication. William Perkins, an English clergyman, was typical, managing to condemn Jews, magical operators and Catholics all in one sentence. 'The Exorcising Jewes, before Christs time...did cast out devils among them, pretending an abilitie to doe this worke in the name of God; whereas in truth, they were all flat Sorcerers, and did it by vertue of a league and compact made with the devill, Which practise...is at this day common and usual among the Popish sort'; and when it came to inflicting the death penalty for any found guilty of practising magic, he was equally trenchant.

As the killing Witch must die by another lawe...so the healing and harmlesse Witch must die by this Law, though he kill not, onely for covenant with Satan. For this must alwaies be remembered as a conclusion, that by Witches we understand not those onely which kill and torment: but all Diviners, Charmers, Juglers, all wizzards, commonly called wise men and wise women: yea, whosoever doe any thing (knowing what they doe) which cannot be effected by nature or art: and in the same number wee reckon all good Witches, which doe no hurt but good, do not spoile and destroy, but save and deliver. (*A Discourse of the Damned Art of Witchcraft*, 1609)

Acquittals

It is commonly supposed that a majority of those who were accused of witchcraft and came before the courts were automatically found guilty and executed. This is, in fact, not so. Given that there were different legal systems in operation within Europe and North America, some depending on the decision of a presiding judge or inquisitor, others upon the voting of a jury, and given that the opportunities for appealing against a guilty verdict also varied within that same geographical spread, it would be unwise to make too many generalisations. But acquittals there were, sometimes on a surprising scale: for example, fifty per cent of the witchcraft cases which came before the High Court of Justiciary in Scotland, whose outcome is recorded, received a 'not guilty' verdict [73, 63].

This figure, however, reminds us to ask what one means when one says 'not guilty'. Scottish evidence from jury trials includes the occasional voting papers which record the individual verdicts of each member of the jury on each item of the indictment, and these reveal that there could be a great deal of dissension within the jury, with some members finding the accused innocent of one item and others finding her or him guilty. More commonly, there was a split, and the final verdict depended on totting up these individual opinions and seeing whether they amounted to an over-all 'guilty' or an over-all 'innocent'. Acquittal could therefore turn on a very small advantage of opinion, but the variation of individual verdicts on separate items suggests that the juries were accustomed to listen carefully to the evidence presented to them and to use local knowledge of local circumstances as well as witnesses' statements in coming to their decisions. Most often it is the absence from the record of this circumstantial information, which makes it difficult for us to appreciate exactly what was going on in the minds of participants in a trial for witchcraft.

An example will illustrate the point. On 21 November 1597, Marjory Mutche was put on trial for witchcraft in Aberdeen.

There were ten items listed in her indictment. Nine of them accused her of inflicting death upon human beings and farm animals, of making one person extremely ill, and of turning another into a cripple: all serious accusations of malefice. The tenth and last item was particularly damaging:

> Thou being confronted with William May within the house of William Brown in Portsoy, he declared in thy face that thou was a manifest witch, in token thereof he showed thy [Devil's] mark under thy left lug in thy neck, and a pin being input therein by the Laird of Esslemont, thou could not feel the same.

Discovery of such a mark, it is commonly assumed, should have been the clinching proof in any attempt to demonstrate that the person accused was undoubtedly a witch. Yet the jury found Marjory not guilty on every count. Her story, therefore, serves as a useful warning to students of witchcraft not to take anything for granted or make too many assumptions.

The Inquisition

The same caveat can be issued when it comes to the Inquisition. Usually thought of as singular and Spanish, the Inquisition in Western Europe consisted of a series of tribunals entrusted with the protection of orthodox faith and the maintenance of ecclesiastical discipline. From the twelfth century onwards, these tribunals were first established in various countries including Spain, Portugal and Italy, and then in the Catholic New World; and after the Protestant reformation they became the subjects of an increasingly hostile propaganda which has left its mark on popular assumption.

Now, when it comes to witchcraft, and indeed magic in general, one needs to realise that the Catholic Church was not so much concerned with magic as such – after all, magic was implicit in the very structure of the created universe as it was conceived during the Middle Ages and early modern period, advances in astronomy notwithstanding – as with heresy and the maintenance of ecclesiastical control over access to and manipulation of powers beyond the purely natural. In consequence, when inquisitors interrogated those who came before them, accused of practising any type of magic, they were interested primarily in finding out whether heresy was involved or not. If it was not, the Inquisition was inclined to lose interest, dismissing the magical operations as nonsense or diabolical illusion. A letter from a senior inquisitor to a provincial official, written in May 1624, expresses this attitude clearly. Witchcraft, he says, has always been considered to be a somewhat dubious activity because it is difficult to prove and is practised mainly by silly women who are taken advantage of by the Devil [136, 205; 116, 25–85].

This is an attitude we have met before in Salazar's investigation of Basque witches during his tour of 1611–12, and owes something to the thirty-two rules for guiding inquisitors in cases of witchcraft, which sprang partly from much earlier Inquisitional policy and partly from Salazar's specific recommendations. We should not, however, misunderstand the Inquisition's scepticism. Its dismissal of popular, widespread magical practices comes from a drive by the whole Church, a drive accentuated after the reforming Council of Trent, to sweep away what it called 'superstition', by which it tended to mean the use of any words, signs, ceremonies or ritual objects not sanctioned by Holy Church herself. It does not imply a wholesale rejection of belief in the reality of magic.

Still, anyone falling under the jurisdiction of the Inquisition could hope to benefit from its official caution and, despite widespread modern belief, from the whole process of inquisitorial investigation and trial, since the Inquisition's procedure for looking into accusations of magic was carefully laid down and hedged with caveats aimed first at discovering the truth of the matter, and secondly at safeguarding the rights of the accused, among which was the right to a legal defence [137]. Scrupulous adherence to these rules could not be guaranteed in every case, of course, especially in provincial tribunals where control from the centre was likely to be weaker, although the case of Malta shows that the Inquisition there was careful to conduct its processes with due attention to legal propriety [27]. Nevertheless, the Inquisitions of Rome and Portugal can be seen to have applied justice with a much lighter hand than the secular courts, largely refraining during the sixteenth century from the use of torture to elicit information; while those of Spain and Rome tended to banish or imprison convicted magical practitioners rather than automatically putting them to death, as was often the case in other European countries [16; 26, 739–40; 102].

Concluding Remarks

The capacity for astonishment (*admiratio*), which we noted earlier as a characteristic of the Middle Ages, did not diminish during the early modern period. There was, indeed, scarcely any reason that it should, as new discoveries in astronomy and geography altered first learned and then, more slowly, general perception of both the heavens and the earth. Explorers and travel-writers regularly used a rhetoric steeped in metaphors of astonishment, and it is perhaps no accident that King Ferdinand of Spain is said to have remarked that Columbus should not have been called 'Admiral' (*Almirante*) but rather 'Wonderer' (*Admirans*) [35, 135–72].

Comets, eclipses and other signs in the sky, dreams, monstrous births, ghosts and other visitations from the realm of spirits, continued to inform the early modern world and provided challenges to theologians, astronomers and natural philosophers as they sought to probe more deeply into the mysteries of creation without stepping over the boundaries of legitimate inquiry [88, 5–65]. Those who did stray beyond the mark, including magical operators of all kinds from the most sophisticated to the most ingenuous, were liable to fall foul of orthodox expectation and tolerance, and thus possibly bring themselves within the compass of the law. For it was not only peasant-witches who were imprisoned or executed. Tommaso Campanella, for example, and Giordano Bruno, both Dominicans with heterodox opinions, suffered the wrath of both religious and secular authorities, Campanella being imprisoned for twenty-seven years, and Bruno burned in Rome on 17 February 1600. But witchcraft in particular, since this was the charge brought against so many magical operators, helped to define a community by drawing public or official boundaries between what was considered normal and what was considered deviant, and thus served, in however dreadful a fashion, to create for people islands of psychological stability in what appeared to be the frightening, protean ocean in which God had required them to live.

But in a world thus encompassed and penetrated by preternatural forces set loose by God's permission and ordered, it seemed, with ever greater independence by the Devil, the temptation to use (whether directly in one's own person or indirectly by means of someone else) those forces for one's own advantage, to solve pressing and immediate problems, clearly proved overwhelming for a majority of people. Few did not consult a magical operator at some time in their lives; few did not employ magic themselves, if only in the shape of an amulet. So were most witches really old women, as claimed by early writers and repeated by modern scholars?

The declaration of Reginald Scot is a *locus classicus*. 'One sort of such as are said to bee witches, are women which be commonly old, lame, blear-eied, pale, fowle, and full of wrinkles; poor, sullen, superstitious, and papists' (*The Discoverie of Witchcraft*, 1584, Book 1, chapter 3). It is worth noting that Scot says 'one sort' of witch is old, thereby implying that there is at least one more which is not, and that this old sort usually consists of Catholics – a purely confessional point. His implication that there existed more than one type of witch, however, reminds us of Stuart Clark's observation that the universe of the early modern period was one of contrariety and inversion. Everything had its opposite; everything was perceived in terms of antithesis [31, 43–79]. The existence of old witches would therefore imply the existence of young witches, and we have come across this pairing already in the literary tradition of young, beautiful/old, ugly handed down from Classical times and its illustration in the pictures of Hans Baldung Grien and Albrecht Dürer. Youth, it appears from at least some literary sources, was regarded as the valid or worthwhile period in a woman's life. Her old age, by contrast, was portrayed as without worth, a time when she was likely to turn antisocial and maleficent [33]. Hence, the contrast between young and old women makes not only an aesthetic comparison, but also moral and sexual points, too: innocence versus corruption, fecundity versus post-menopausal barrenness.

So, in spite of its being true that constant hard physical labour and child-bearing were likely to age a woman's appearance prematurely: and that very frequently the indictments of witches refer to their having practised magic for ten, twenty or even thirty years, so that if the women were 'old' when they were arrested, they had not been old when they had started to practise their craft: we must look very carefully at any literary or pictorial evidence which suggests that a witch was usually a crone. These sources are not photographic records. They were written or limned for a purpose, and that purpose may well have been informed by any number of non-realistic considerations.

6

Witches in the North and East

Large-scale prosecution of witches broke out in southern Germany during the last decades of the sixteenth century and from there spread, like ripples from the broken surface of a pool, to the further edges of Europe. North and East especially witnessed their major outbreaks in the second half of the seventeenth century or even later, with Sweden seeing its worst period of trials in 1668–9, Poland between 1675 and 1700 and Hungary in 1728–9. There was magical practice and there were witches in all these places well before the authorities felt obliged to prosecute practitioners in sizeable numbers.

Why there should have been such a delay in comparison with southern Europe is therefore an interesting question. Klaniczay has suggested that the principal reason for this delay may be found in the late arrival in those areas of an economic, social and cultural evolution which came to the West perhaps a century earlier; and he also points to the relaxation of intolerable tensions caused by wars or uprisings, which enabled people to consider the outcome of the violence they had undergone, and look for possible causes of their recent suffering [68, 224]. In Sweden, for example, imperial expansion in the seventeenth century led to the growth of a new bourgeoisie in her provincial towns, and these tended to regard the surrounding peasants as both stupid and dangerous. From 1664, therefore, a new moral code was inflicted from above, in which many manifestations of popular culture were reinterpreted as classical witch-theory suggested they should be, and in consequence of that the 1670s saw a notable outbreak of witchcraft trials [5, 293–4].

But while this idea may apply quite well to Sweden or parts of Hungary, it does not sit well with Poland which was more open to the transmission of demonological theory from Germany, and one explanation for the late crudescence of witch-trials there is that war with Sweden and Russia before 1655 and 1660 prevented her from dealing with anything else. Another is the rise of a more militant Catholicism after 1648, which sought (as elsewhere) to impose religious orthodoxy where it had either not existed before or had been merely luke-warm; and a third is the late transference of witchcraft from her ecclesiastical to her secular jurisdiction, usually more rigorous and often less well trained in the law, especially in provincial courts [**78**, *196–8*]. The reasons for delay, therefore, like witchcraft itself, are complex and one should not make the mistake of trying to find a single, overarching explanation for either.

Scandinavia

Christianity came late to the peoples of Northern Europe. Serious missionary work began there in about the middle of the ninth century and during the tenth Nordic kings were actively encouraging their subjects to become Christian. Nevertheless, the native religions were not immediately, or even quickly, displaced and much of their belief and practice remained to coexist first with Catholicism and then later with the faiths of the Protestant reformation. Christian literature, as one might expect, tried to relegate Scandinavia's pagan past to a distant antiquity, although it was very well aware that reality was neither as straightforward nor as comfortable as that. Olaus Magnus, Archbishop of Uppsala, for example, devoted Book 3 of his monumental *History of the Peoples of the North* (1555) to a description of the 'superstitious worship of evil spirits' and 'gross errors' which had quite literally bedevilled the Scandinavians, Lithuanians and Finns before they were converted, and although much of his account is woven from the works of Roman and Scandinavian writers and set in what appears to be the distant past, every so often it lapses into descriptions of what magicians or witches still do in the present, as when he says that witches, 'of whom there are very many in the North', should be punished by burning.

Initially, Mediaeval Norwegian, Danish and Swedish experiences of witchcraft tended to follow the general European pattern, in as much as their laws seem to have winked at beneficent magic and regarded witchcraft principally as the practice of *maleficium*. So it may be that absence from Nordic witchcraft during this period of the southern European theory of the Sabbat prevented judicial severity from infecting official attitudes to magic as a whole. But once that theory, along with its attendant assumptions and ramifications, had penetrated Northern Europe, of course, the situation changed; and the union of the Norwegian and Danish crowns, followed in 1536 by the relegation of Norway to the status of Danish province, also meant that thereafter Norway's treatment of witches became one with that of Denmark.

Nevertheless, Scandinavian law was not entirely benign when it came to dealing with witches, and one can see quite clearly a hardening of attitude between the eleventh century when statute law condemned to exile those found guilty of practising witchcraft, and the same law two centuries later which now prescribed capital punishment instead. The reason for this increased severity appears to be the later overt association of witchcraft with heresy, and a case from early fourteenth-century Bergen links both of these with illicit sexual behaviour and worship of Satan. Indeed, the link between witchcraft and sexual licence became so strong that in Swedish the phrase 'witch house' was a common term for 'brothel' [91].

The Protestant reformation, too, along with the spread of Neo-platonic ideas in intellectual circles, which encouraged interest in natural magic, also seems to have brought about a hardening of attitudes and made the authorities of both Church and state increasingly suspicious of all forms of magical activity. This took time to filter through into the judicial process, but the 1600s saw Sweden, for example, extend capital punishment to include those found guilty of any form of magical operation, not just those designated 'witchcraft', with the lower courts, as one might expect, applying the death penalty more often than the higher, a trend which continued into the eighteenth century [133, 70–2]. The principal reason for this extension we have seen before: magic, witchcraft, sorcery, and all forms of 'superstition' were considered to have a common denominator – their dependence on an explicit or implicit pact with Satan – which rendered their activities fundamentally idolatrous.

A number of trials during the seventeenth century in the north of Norway, in a region now known as East Finnmark, will serve to illustrate the way in which traditional magic was charged alongside or designated as 'witchcraft', with devastating results for those who were brought to court. The area had a mixed population of Sami and non-Sami, with the former having a very widespread reputation as workers of magic. This magic involved acts of malefice such as raising contrary winds and sinking ships at sea, and driving away fish from the shore, as well as curative magical operations for both humans and animals, raising favourable winds, lifting bewitchment and bestowing various kinds of blessing. But between 1652 and 1663, a series of witch-trials which included several children among the defendants, (the youngest aged eight), saw added to accusations of this nature the diabolic pact, shape-changing, attendance at the Sabbat and sexual intercourse with the Devil resulting in the birth of an evil spirit in human guise. Torture, sometimes specified as the cold-water ordeal, sometimes unspecified, was used in order to elicit the necessary confessions, not all of which, however, were adhered to after the torture had ceased.

What we see here, then, very clearly is European witchcraft theory reaching out to embrace Sami magical beliefs and practices, and the courts being equally severe on both. What is perhaps unusual about these trials is that, although most of the defendants were women, most of the men who were charged were Sami, whereas most of the women were not; and in spite of the fact that the Sami women involved were accused of malefice, it was their menfolk who were especially targeted by the authorities. Yet the men's confessions do not involve attendance at a Sabbat nor any pact with the Devil. The men, it seems, were prosecuted largely for working old-fashioned, 'pagan' magic, while the women were drawn into the specific witchcraft charges common to the rest of Western and Southern Europe [146].

Most of those charged during these trials in Finnmark were sentenced to death. Scandinavian legal procedures, however, like those of the Inquisition, could offer some degrees of assurance to the accused. These were the existence of juries; torture was used sparingly; courts were more interested in whether specific acts of malefice had been done than in compacts with the Devil; those accused of witchcraft were allowed to bring suits for defamation against their accusers; and there was provision for appeal to a higher court [94, 428–9]. Nevertheless, these provisions were not enough to protect every defendant during those periods when official animus was directed with special severity against workers of magic, and in Denmark perhaps half those tried were executed, while in Norway the number seems to have been just a little less, 280–300 out of a total of 750 [12, 551–7; 100; 63]. Even the provision of safeguards, therefore, was no guarantee against local outbreaks which may have been restricted in location and in time, but were still oppressive and potentially devastating to the communities in which they happened.

Iceland

The reception of Christianity in Iceland can be dated to *c*.1000 and the new religion remained tolerant of magic – indeed, Catholic bishops and priests both possessed and used books of magic, in spite of the twelfth-century law code, the *Grágás*, which ordained outlawry for anyone found guilty of practising harmful magic – until the Protestant reformation arrived, after which many aspects of magical activity were reinterpreted as witchcraft and legal process against its practitioners began. Even that took time. Witches were not convicted as 'witches' until the seventeenth century, and trials tended to be concentrated in the north-west of the country where Danish law was paramount.

The vocabulary of these trials was rooted in that of Western Europe, with the accusations resting upon an assumption of *maleficium*; and it may well not be a coincidence that Jón Rögnvaldson, the first person to be executed for 'witchcraft', (that is to say, for magical activity designated as this alien crime), was tried by an official well acquainted with the *Malleus Maleficarum*. Rögnvaldson was burned in 1625. He had been accused by a sick boy of causing his illness by magic, and when his house was searched the officials discovered a sheet of paper on which were written runes, the signs or characters common to Icelandic divination. (The word *rún* means 'secret'.) So it is clear that Rögnvaldson was actually no witch in the new prosecutory sense, but more of an old-style diviner.

Icelandic magicians, then, male or female, while practising the full range of magic one finds elsewhere in Western Europe, had certain beliefs and practices of their own. Skaldic verse embodied the magical power of chanted words and represented the essence of Icelandic magic which depended largely on specialist knowledge of how to use magical vocabulary, whether written or spoken. Magicians could also seek advice from trolls, the spirits of water or earth, who inhabited specific locales, and also from ghosts whom they often conjured with the help of the bones of corpses they had disinterred.

The case of Jón laerdi Gudmundsson (*c*.1574–1658) illustrates some of these points. He was a man of various talents including painting and scholarship who specialised in exorcising ghosts by chanting magical songs, and became famous for this skill. But he had the ill luck to fall foul of his local clergyman and was eventually tried for witchcraft on two general charges: (1) he carried out magical exorcisms, and (2) he possessed manuscripts containing instructions for magical operations. Jón was found guilty but outlawed instead of being put to death, and the clergyman was defrocked because his motive for bringing the accusation was fuelled by malice. Jón's activities, we may notice, had nothing to do with classical witchcraft theory. He was condemned on the standard assumption that they were underpinned by reliance on some kind of pact with Satan [**56**, *197–243*; **57**; **97**].

Interestingly enough, during Catholic times, the authorities did not express too much concern over attempted consultations with the dead. It was not until after the Protestant reformation with its rejection of the doctrine of Purgatory and its obsessive desire to root out 'superstition' and Catholicism that there seems to have been some kind of revitalisation of the practice, as though the Icelanders, faced with a challenge to deny and destroy one of their most deeply held beliefs, were determined to fight it off and defend their psyches.

Other notable features of Icelandic witch-trials were the absence of any notion of the Sabbat or belief in the Devil's marks, and of the use of the water test; and whereas the sagas had tended to designate mothers who were especially close to their sons as possible workers of magic on their behalf, in the later trials it was men who were preponderant among the accused: 110 out of 120 defendants, with 21 out of 22 burned for witchcraft [**42**; **53**]. By and large, however, the number of trials was small and those accused of witchcraft are likely to have benefited from a Danish ordinance of 1617 which decreed that only those who had made a pact with Satan were to be executed. Cunning folk were simply to be exiled – hence Jón Gudmundsson's lucky escape from burning.

Of Scandinavian witchcraft as a whole, then, it may be said that apart from one or two untypical, localised convulsions, there was no intensive prosecution of witches, and that those bursts of severity which did happen took place largely after their equivalents further south. It also seems clear that authorities in Scandinavia and Iceland took their cue from those southern examples, and that the arrival of Protestantism made a significant difference, not quite so marked in countries further south, to the relative tolerance

hitherto shown to magical operators, by designating many historical native beliefs and practices as witchcraft in accordance with a
witchcraft theory which had been formulated for somewhat different times and cultures.

Russia

There was, as Russell Zguta has pointed out, only a fine line
between witchcraft and medicine in Russia before the advent of
Peter the Great, and since it was believed that most illnesses were
caused by maleficent magic, it followed that they could be cured
only by magic, the most favoured means being the *zagovor*, the
magical incantation. Nothing illustrates more clearly the double-
edged power of magic, for the *zagovor* could be used both to bring
illness and to cure it, and so popular was its use that when Tsar
Alexis issued a decree in 1648, aimed at the elimination of all superstitious beliefs and practices among the people, he was careful to
mention the *zagovor* as deserving of special condemnation [150; 121,
165–201].

Maleficent magic was feared and punished by burning, the victims, as in Iceland and Finland, being men rather more often than
women. The arrival of famine in a neighbourhood tended to see
magical operators blamed, accused of causing it through *maleficia*,
and put to death for their crime against the community, as happened in Suzdal in 1024 and Rostov in 1071. Plague was another
disaster which might set off persecution, and it is possible that this
accounts for the burning of twelve female witches at Pskov in 1411,
although the incident coincides with an attempt by Metropolitan
Fotii to eradicate all forms of magical practice and remnants of
paganism from the region under his control.

The efforts of the ecclesiastical establishment to Christianise the
people more thoroughly, however, had little of the success the
clergy were hoping for, and the Stoglov Church Council of 1551
was obliged to debate, at the immediate instance of Tsar Ivan
IV, what should be done about witches and other magical practitioners. The Council recommended that such persons be executed
by the state, but the Tsar chose to ignore this, issuing instead in
1552 a decree that everyone must henceforth cease to have any
dealing with occult specialists of any kind and that witches would
be tried by civil as well as ecclesiastical courts. This ensured

that religious considerations alone would not govern their arrest and trial.

The Tsar's interest in the subject was undoubtedly stimulated by the recent history of magical attempts against members of the Imperial family, Ivan III's first wife having been killed by maleficent magic in 1467, and a subsequent wife having conspired with witches to poison him by a form of magic known as *veneficium*. Likewise, the second half of the sixteenth century saw accusations of harmful magic almost regularly enter the realm of politics, with the current Tsar either as the object of magical conspiracies or as a complainant against the magic of others who wished to harm him [**149**].

But it was the seventeenth century which saw what might be called the high point of Russian witch-prosecution, with continuing investigations and trials in the highest political and social circles, and the Tsars trying to weed out occult practices throughout the populace with threats of knouting and exile. Even so, the numbers of those who died appear to have been small. In Moscow, for example, 99 people were accused between 1622 and 1700, of whom only about 19 or 20 were condemned to death, although one must bear in mind that Russia was, as it still is, vast and that records when available have scarcely been examined. The impression of absence of widespread prosecution may, therefore, be mistaken [**12**, *547–8*].

It is clear, however, that Russian witchcraft lacked certain essential characteristics of its Western counterpart, such as the Sabbat and worship of Satan, and this made its trials peculiar to itself. Zguta has suggested that the continuous coexistence of paganism and Christianity in Russia, a phenomenon which, as we have seen, both Church and state tried several times to rectify without much success, meant that Russian witches could be tried and punished for malefice but not for heresy, a feature of Russian law which made all the difference to whether or not one trial would lead to others and thus start a constantly growing chain of fatalities.

Hungary and Poland

Large-scale prosecutions came late to Hungary. The most intense period lasted for about forty years, between 1710 and 1750, when 809 people were put on trial and 213 were executed. There had been a surge in the previous two decades (1690–1710) when 209 stood trial and 85 were executed, but before that the evidence seems to suggest that trials were comparatively few – twenty-five during the period 1590–1610, for example, when southern Germany was suffering some of its worst judicial excesses. The magical crimes of which these people were accused, however, are familiar, for unlike their Russian counterparts, Hungarian indictments included references to the diabolic pact, the Devil's mark, and attendance at the Sabbat, with a description of the latter dating as far back as 1574. Perhaps not surprisingly, the evidence comes from confessions made by witches living not far from the Austrian border, or from German communities inside Hungary [68, 222, 249–50].

But while certain features of their beliefs and practices were peculiar to themselves – witches, it is said, were organised as though they were an army, with Satan as their commander-in-chief – just as had happened in other parts of Europe, the cunning person, known in Hungarian as a *táltos*, a combination of shaman and magical operator, began to appear as a defendant in witch-trials even though he or she was actually an enemy of witches. These people possessed special skills which enabled them to cure ill-nesses, look for buried treasure and utter prophecies; but, as is the usual way with magic, they were also credited with the ability to interfere with crops and work other kinds of harm – hence their amalgamation with witches in official perceptions [78, 198; 38; 68, 244–9; 109, 134–43]. Still, as Klaniczay points out, the *táltos* did not play a major part in Hungarian witch-trials. The trials themselves displayed a remarkable diversity in both their accusers and their defendants. Transylvania, for example, experienced religious tensions during the sixteenth century, with Lutherans, Calvinists, Unitarians, and Jesuits struggling for people's souls. 'Each religious party', says Klaniczay, 'advocated an increasing hostility towards manifestations of early modern popular culture...the effect of which is shown here by the fact that the accused mostly came under suspicion for having performed traditional fertility rites or healing magic' [69, 158]. Then, in the seventeenth century, Transylvania saw a different kind of witch-trial in which its aristocratic families accused each other's women of witchcraft as a normal means of conducting political or conspiratorial discourse. In the western part of the country, however, it was principally men – shepherds and vagrant magical operators – who found themselves charged as witches. Shepherds, as we saw earlier in the cases from Normandy, constituted a social group often associated with the practice of magic and thus liable to be accused of witchcraft if local circumstances dictated an outbreak of prosecutions. In their indictments, shepherds were often associated with werewolves, but as this is not a concept actually native to Hungarian folklore, one must suppose that these stories told of them originally came from elsewhere. Finally, one should note that children quite frequently appeared as accusers in Hungarian witchcraft trials, sometimes bringing charges against members of their own families, sometimes against their employers [68, 239], a situation which is reminiscent of Swedish trials of the second half of the seventeenth century, in which children accused their parents or other adults of taking them to a Sabbat on Mount Blåkulla.

Now, while it is true that Hungary's witch-trials were particularly frequent at the beginning of the eighteenth century, they need to be put into some kind of perspective. In the worst four decades, 1710–50, an average of twenty people were accused each year, of whom we know that five or six were executed and three or four acquitted (fines and unknown outcomes accounting for the rest). These figures are not excessive, given the size of the country. Witchcraft trials were often concentrated in one city, such as those which took place in Szeged in 1728, the defendants, accusers and witnesses all being drawn either from the same community or from communities nearby. The effect of these trials on the immediate area could, therefore, be severe but their taking place does not imply that a whole province or country was devastated or even involved. This, of course, applies to any country in Europe, but it is worth bearing in mind when one looks at witchcraft in Poland, where a reputed 5,000 or more legal executions are alleged to have taken place between 1676 and 1725 (although Levack considers this total somewhat high [78, 195]). That gives a figure of about 100 executions per year, a stark contrast with Hungary's five or six.

One reason for Poland's apparent greater severity rests on her transfer of responsibility for trying witchcraft cases from the ecclesiastical to the civil courts in 1658. The secular arm was much more severe than that of the Church, and the autonomy exercised by local courts meant that any impetus to prosecute was difficult, if not impossible, to restrain. The abuses which could result may be seen from a pastoral letter written by Casimir Czartoriski, Bishop of Cujavia and Pomerania, dated 11 April 1669. In it he complains that many judges were credulous and too ready to torture suspects, while ignoring the stringent rules which were supposed to govern any application of torture. But suspects continued to be tortured, he says, until they acknowledged as their accomplices in magic those people whose names the torturers suggested to them. Any who died in prison during or as a result of their torture were denied Christian burial and treated as though they had already been found guilty. 'The principal cause of such errors', Czartoriski adds, 'is that judgement of witches is in the hands of men who can scarcely read or write.'

His strictures undoubtedly help to explain why certain regions in Poland witnessed a particular cruelty against suspect witches, but they also have a wider application; for while boorish and vicious behaviour such as he describes may not have been uniform all over the West [135], there is evidence from elsewhere that what he criticised in Polish provincial judges could also have been said of similar officials in many other parts of Europe.

7
Witches in the New World

The Dwelling-place of Satan

Europeans did not arrive in the New World without any preconceptions of what such a world might be like. For years the white strangers had been brought up on certain types of literature which stressed that on the fringes of civilisation as they knew it existed weird and fabulous people and creatures, inhabiting extraordinary, wonderful lands where nothing was quite as it was in everyday Europe. The principal sources of these notions were fantasists such as Mandeville, and the ancient Roman encyclopaedist Pliny the Elder whose multi-volumed work had never gone out of print, so to speak, and was constantly appearing in fresh, annotated editions. But there were many others – Pomponius Mela, Solinus, Isidore of Seville, Vincent de Beauvais, to name but a few, not to mention Peter Martyr and later the illustrator Théodore de Bry – whose works encouraged Europeans to expect the unusual and the fantastic rather than the norm in remote parts of the world [20].

How, then, did the European conquerors, priests and traders cope with venturing into such strange and potentially perilous places? Essentially they had two ways in which they could assimilate and explain to themselves what it was they were seeing and meeting. One was to turn to the tradition of Classical literature which had, in part, told them beforehand what to expect. Analogy would help them to comprehend and therefore to make appropriate responses. A second was to see the New World in terms of the Christian European analogue, and here one notes that the Spaniards tended to employ the vocabulary of 'otherness', which they already used at home, to describe what they found there. Thus, for example, Inca temples were often referred to as 'mosques', and Inca myths could be reinterpreted by reference to European demonic theories [81, *108, 117–19*; 28, *32–3*; 82]. The consequences of these two possible attitudes were profoundly different. On the one hand there were those who were prepared to say that the Amerindians equalled, or even surpassed, the Greeks and Romans in cultural achievements and lived in what was essentially a pagan Golden Age; and on the other there were those who viewed the native peoples as being slaves by nature, in league with the Devil, and guilty of the most appalling crimes perpetrated both against nature and against God.

Now, it has been said that early visitors to the New World had only three interests in the local peoples they met: material gain, sexual gratification and religious conversion. It is not part of my task to comment on the first two, but let us examine a little more closely the urge to draw the Amerindians into the Christian fold. Many of the Spanish friars referred to the native gods as 'demons' or 'devils' or 'evil spirits' – 'I have mostly seen them with a tail and feet like our Satan', said one – and to their temples as 'houses of Hell', recording their views in drawings to accompany their books for publication back home, drawings which made it quite clear to their readers how such gods were to be regarded [20, 67–83]. As a result of such descriptions, whether verbal or pictorial, a view was formed by those who had never been to the New World: the natives who lived there were not only primitive, but wicked. Who could believe anything else with the evidence of such drawings before them, and descriptions of the human sacrifices with which the idols were worshipped and placated? Did not Gioseffo di Acosta write in 1591, in his *Natural and Moral History of the Indies*, of 'their child-murdering initiations, their secret mysteries, their orgies with outlandish ceremonies...everywhere a welter of blood and murder, theft and fraud, corruption, treachery, riots, perjury, disturbance, pollution of souls, and sins against nature'? The anointing of their priests, he said, was carried out with a substance compounded of every sort of poisonous vermin such as spiders, scorpions, snakes and centipedes which, when burned and mixed with an hallucinogenic herb, had the power of turning newly ordained priests into witches who saw the Devil and visited him by night in dark and sinister mountains and caves. Satanic pollution and filth, he declared, invaded every corner of these people's religion. Indeed, their religion was nothing but an inverted parody of the true faith, the ultimate expression of idolatry – charges which the learned of Europe were regularly bringing against their own witches and magical operators.

This reaction should not be surprising. In the sixteenth century, Spanish settlers began pouring into the American colonies, and part of the cultural baggage they brought with them was an intimate personal knowledge of magic and witchcraft, 'personal' because they would certainly have come across both at home at some time in their lives, and the solutions used at home to deal with these occult workers. It is also perfectly possible that a large number of the visitors would have used and continued to be ready to use magical practices to help them cope with the stresses and problems of their new, tense and sometimes dangerous situation. Not only did they expect to find fabled monsters, giants, bearded women, dragons and all the other denizens of Classical learning and Mediaeval romance, they also presumed they would come across Satan himself, his attendant angels, evil spirits of all kinds and those earthly followers of evil, witches and magicians; and whereas monsters may not have emerged, contact with the Amerindians actually did confirm the view that Satan lived in the New World [**113**, *151–64*]. For the native Americans also had their workers of various kinds of magic, and these people were usually held in high esteem, credited with the power not only to cure illnesses and carry out the commands of their various gods, but also to change themselves into animals, fly through the air and cause sickness or death as required. Ready-made parallels between Amerindian and European magic and witchcraft, therefore, presented themselves to the settlers and confirmed their worst expectations [**81**, *112*, *115–16*].

Needless to say, these cunning folk and popular magicians elicited both misunderstanding and deep suspicion in the foreign invaders. But every so often there arose from among the various missionary orders which came to convert the Amerindian a holy man who either worked miracles himself or with whom miracles were associated. Such people were known in Spanish as *venerables*, and they were credited with being masters of the natural elements, keeping away storms, commanding the clouds and the plants, lighting or putting out fires at will, and devoting themselves to prophecy and divination. Above all, they were believed to multiply miraculous healings both before and after their death, since their bodies, quickly dismembered by the faithful to provide relics, were also endowed with miraculous powers. Now in what way, one is bound to ask, did these *venerables* differ from the indigenous *curanderos* who also worked cures, or from the *conjuradores de nubes* who made it rain or made the hail stay away, and ruled the mountains as if the vast space of the sky and the winds were under their command [28, 58–62]? All exercised the same therapeutic and climatic function, the same faculty, above all, of communicating with the divine by means of a dream or a vision. Yet who called the *venerables* sorcerers, or the *curanderos* saints? Which party was practising religion and which magic?

A similar problem of interpretation in relation to cunning folk was met by demonologists and theologians in Europe, too, and their answer, as we have seen, frequently involved attempts at suppression of their activities, sometimes on charges of simple illicit magic, sometimes by reinterpreting their magical operations as witchcraft and charging them with that. Just so, the *curanderos* of New Spain were investigated by the Inquisition, for fear that what they were doing constituted a form of activity which was all too liable to lapse into idolatry. Some *curanderos* accused themselves, others were denounced, and torture was employed to secure or confirm confessions. But if they were found guilty, the *curanderos* were not handed over to the secular arm to be put to death. Instead, their punishment was retained in the hands of the Inquisition which administered it in two different forms. First, there came a private warning and a prohibition against their continuing their magical practices; secondly, they were required to appear in public, gagged, carrying candles, and wearing tunics which were covered in symbols which made it clear what their offences had been. The penitents also wore nooses about their necks and had their crimes broadcast by the town crier [112]. It was a procedure significantly similar to that used in Spain in cases of abjuring heretics.

Why, then, did magical operators continue to exercise their various skills? Because they fulfilled a genuine need. Nor was it only the Amerindians who practised magic. A colonial society is, by its nature, institutionally rigid and hierarchical, and therefore magic offers a means of redressing the inequities to which domination of one group of people by another will inevitably give rise. In the New World, an enormous number of people found magic a comfort in their distress or a means of taking revenge for the wrongs they suffered or thought they suffered – the Amerindians first of all; then later African slaves; all those born of mixed race; Europeans who failed to make their fortunes and stayed on to become a particular under-class; orphans; widows and abandoned wives, many of whom took to prostitution as the only means whereby they might earn their daily bread. Some of their magical practices were modelled on Catholic liturgy and, as priests often complained, misused not only holy oil, the church altar and other sacred objects, but even the Host itself. Others distorted Christian prayers, and yet others adapted the model of the European witch, her pact with the Devil, her nocturnal flights and the Sabbat. Wherever the authorities looked, then, they would be sure to find what they were looking for, and would be able to recognise it by reference to the European experience.

New England

It is important to remember, however, that it was not only Catholics who colonised the New World. Protestant privateers, on the one hand, made war against the Spanish Empire, and their co-religionist audience back in Europe was quickly presented with such books as Jean de Léry's *Histoire du Brésil*, Urbain Chauveton's *Histoire Nouvelle du Nouveau Monde*, and Théodore de Bry's *Grands Voyages*, all of which formed a Huguenot corpus with two principal messages to convey: (1) the crimes of the Spanish conquest, and (2) the sufferings of the Noble Savage whom the cruel Spanish (i.e., Catholics) should have left in his native ignorance, since his forcible conversion to Catholicism was almost worse than eternal damnation. Lavishly illustrated with pictures which did more to promote these messages than the text itself [32], these books helped to initiate a strain of historiography in which the Catholic superstition and fanaticism was contrasted with Protestant reason to the ultimate benefit of the innocent and oppressed Amerindian; and so, not for the first time, the history of magic was used for the purposes of confessional propaganda.

Further north, however, in New England, this version of events was not repeated, perhaps for the simple reason that it was there too close to the bone. For the Puritan settlers of New England saw themselves as the equivalent of God's chosen people, the Israelites, and thus, by analogy, the native Americans round them as the Canaanites, Assyrians and Babylonians of biblical history, to be treated at once with violence and contempt [123, 3–4, 220–5]; and just as the Spanish had seen New Spain as Satan's habitation, so the Puritans of the north located him in the territories they had taken over and were trying to control. Thus, three people from Virginia, all writing in 1613, made that same basic point. Henry Spelman observed that the American Indians for the most part worshipped the Devil (*Relation of Virginea*), as did William Crashaw who said that 'Satan visibly and palpably reigns there, more than in any other known place of the world' (*New-yeeres Gift to Virginea*); while the minister of Henrico, Alexander Whitaker, wrote to the Council and Company of Virginia, resident in England,

> Let the miserable condition of these naked slaves of the divell move you to compassion toward them. They acknowledge that there is a great good God, but know him not, having the eyes of their understanding as yet blinded: wherefore they serve the divell for feare, after a most base manner, sacrificing (as I have heere heard) their owne Children to him: I have sent one Image of their god to the Counsell in *England*, which is painted upon one side of a toad-stoole, much like unto a deformed monster. Their Priests . . . are no other but such as our English Witches are.
>
> (*Good Newes from Virginia*)

Nor did the passage of time make much difference to these sentiments, for in 1692 we find the Boston minister, Cotton Mather, asserting, 'I believe there never was a poor Plantation more pursued by the *Wrath* of the *Devil* than our poor *New-England* . . . It was a rousing *alarm* to the Devil, when a great Company of English *Protestants* and *Puritans* came to erect Evangelical Churches in a corner of the World where he had reign'd without any control for many Ages' (*The Wonders of the Invisible World*).

These, and many other remarks of a like kind, were not only patronising: they were ingenuous. For the Europeans who had emigrated to the New World brought with them a freight of magical baggage from their own countries, and if they were not themselves practitioners, they knew perfectly well how witches, magicians and cunning folk operated back at home. Indeed, their very journey to the New World almost certainly reminded them at some point of the magic they may have thought they had left behind, since the sailors on board their ship would have resorted to magic in order to conjure a good wind or dispel a storm in accordance with their need; and the Puritan emigrant minister, Thomas Shepard, recorded that when the crew on his vessel, the *Hope*, became convinced they were suffering severe storms because their ship was bewitched, they nailed two red-hot horse shoes to the main mast to

discover the culprit and counteract her or his malefice [34, 165–6].
Not without reason, then, does John Demos make the important
point that, whereas the native peoples tended to be categorised as
Devil-worshippers rather than witches (despite the terminology to
which the colonists often resorted), when it came to uncovering
witches in the European sense of the word, New Englanders turned
to their own communities and found them there, where they
expected them to be [37, 71].

So, once arrived in the New World, the emigrants proceeded with
their plan to establish a godly, patriarchal society. This, by definition, provided only a subordinate role for women whose expected
behaviour was based to some extent on a number of carefully chosen
biblical figures such as Susannah, notable for her chastity, and Sarah
and Hannah, models of female patience. These examples were
important for the ministers and magistrates of the new communities
because part of the psychological luggage they had brought with
them from Europe was a belief in women's latent propensity to evil,
an inclination to sin and a weakness in the face of diabolical temptation which all too often manifested themselves as monstrous births
or possession by evil spirits [65, 160–79; 144, 53–61]. Witches, of
course, provided further examples of Satan's prevailing over the
frailty of women, particularly young women, and many New England theologians were directly influenced by the work of the English
Puritan William Perkins. Cotton Mather, for example, included 'An
Abstract of Mr. Perkins's Way for the Discovery of Witches' in his
1692 witchcraft tract – whose animadversions upon the diabolic pact
clearly articulated the Puritan point of view:

> Witchcraft signifies all curious arts, wrought by the operation of
> the devill.... The ground is a league or compact with the
> Devill.... If by true faith wee make a covenant with God; then a
> false faith, in the use of Satanicall ceremonies, makes a covenant
> with the devill. And without this, there is no practice of witch-
> craft.
> (*A Commentary upon the Epistle to the Galatians* (1604), chapter 5)

Perkins also lays out the range of magical arts subsumed under
this definition: divination, 'juggling' (by which he meant prestidigitation), and the use of charms or incantation to inflict or cure
illness. They are exactly what one might expect, and are found in
abundance in the court records of New England [55; 50, 24–54].

The numbers of those accused, however, cannot be described as large. Westerkamp puts it at 344 between 1620 and 1725. A majority of them were women (78 per cent) and when 103 came to trial, the proportion of women was even greater (86 per cent), with a good many of the men accused drawn in because they were related, usually indeed the husbands of the suspects. Property may have furnished a key to some of the accusations. It is a remarkable feature of the New England suspects that many of the women had inherited property from their fathers or husbands, and could therefore be seen as a threat to the patriarchy which informed their communities. Elizabeth Godman, for example, a widow from New Haven in Connecticut, was accused of witchcraft twice, in 1653 and 1655. The charges were those of causing sickness in people and animals, inflicting death upon them, and having a preternatural ability to foretell the future; and it is noteworthy that one of the chief complainants against her was her landlord, Stephen Goodyear, the deputy governor of the colony, who owed her the not inconsiderable sum of £152 at the time of his death in 1658, and who told the court that she was in possession of property sufficient for her needs, a remark he clearly felt compelled to make in view of her habit of scrounging buttermilk and beer from some of her neighbours [55, 61–73; **65**, *305 n.6*].

Most of the New England trials, however, belong to only two outbreaks of prosecution. One of these took place in Hartford, Connecticut, between 1662 and 1665 when nine women and four men were accused in connection with the diabolical possession of a woman, Ann Cole, and the sickness of an 8-year-old girl, Elizabeth Kelly. Three of the women and one of the men were put on trial, found guilty and executed. The second outbreak took place in and around Salem, Massachusetts, between 1692 and 1693 and involved 185 persons, of whom 27 were convicted and 19 executed. Here, too, the principal charge was one of causing diabolical possession in some of the accusers, and in fact, as Carol Karlsen has pointed out, in spite of their notoriety, the Salem trials were not essentially different from others which preceded them. It was the number of people involved, and the vicious tensions which had been festering in the neighbourhood for the previous twenty years, which gave Salem its initial claim to fame and make it loom overlarge in the history of witchcraft in New England [**65**, *35–40*; **37**, *58–9*]. Later claims, of course, rest partly upon the unusual abundance of its surviving records, and partly upon the play by Arthur Miller, *The*

Crucible (1953), written during the heat of Senator McCarthy's trawl for Communists in American society, and his later film script which took even more liberties with the facts than his stage-play had done.

But while Salem was the last major outbreak of witch prosecution in New England, witchcraft and the practice of magic did not disappear from the country. As late as 1802, for example, a youth was tried and convicted in New York for attempting to undo a witch's malefice against him by trying to cut her three times on the forehead, an incident which was by no means the last manifestation of its kind.

Canada

When Jesuit missionaries came to Canada, they were both fascinated and alarmed by the shamanic culture they encountered there. The Superior of the Canadian mission in 1632, Father Paul Le Jeune, used military terminology in his reports, describing the territory round the St. Lawrence as 'Satan's empire', and his principal aim as being that of destroying the huge numbers of Indian superstitions which he viewed as potential enemy spoils he would eventually dedicate to Christ. The native shamans were therefore chief among the Jesuits' targets [7, 91–6]. But curiously enough, the Indians reciprocated by regarding the missionaries themselves as shamans – indeed, some Hurons had themselves baptised either in the hope of thereby escaping hostile Jesuit magic, or of learning from the missionaries how they might become better magicians – and in consequence it was not long before both sides entered, as it were, a magical battle, rather like that between Moses and Pharaoh's magicians, to determine whose magic was the more powerful.

A major opportunity for each party to demonstrate its abilities was provided by a series of plague epidemics which broke out between 1634 and 1641. The Hurons were convinced that the plague had two causes: (a) the Jesuits who were originating and spreading the disease out of sheer malicious exercise of harmful magic, and (b) a number of their own people who had offended against Huron canons of generosity and acceptable social behaviour. Some of these last were tortured by the Huron war chiefs, since it was believed that torture destroyed their magical power – an interesting parallel with the European theory that when a witch was arrested she often lost her contact with Satan, who then abandoned her to her fate, and thus could no longer operate any form of magic. The Jesuits, for their part, turned to religious ritual (as well as straightforward medical remedies) to confront the plague, only to find that the Hurons regarded these rites as shamanistic and borrowed or adapted parts of them in order to bolster their own magical efforts [138, 245–7; 98, 30–3; 7, 97–8].

But magic was not found or experienced simply by contact with the native peoples. French immigrants brought with them their own European heritage of beliefs and practice, just as their English-speaking counterparts elsewhere in North America, and in Quebec we find a wide range of examples whose magical content should now be familiar to us. A 16-year-old servant girl, Barbe Hallé, was troubled by what sounds like a poltergeist at the end of 1660. As many as twenty people in her vicinity saw stones appear out of nowhere, flying past them without doing any harm but with a great deal of noise and force. Hallé was the only person to see the cause of these and other manifestations, a large number of evil spirits who appeared to her in their own likeness and under the guise of men, women, children and animals. They also took her over in acts of possession and spoke through her mouth without actually seeming to make visible use of it. Finally, she was removed to the Hospitaller Convent in Quebec where she was put under the charge of Mother Catherine of St Augustine and eventually recovered.

Mother Catherine was the ideal spiritual physician to help young Hallé, for we are told that Satan and other evil spirits regularly visited her, especially between 1661 and 1667, and she therefore became inured to demonic sights and sounds. One peculiar incident happened to her at the end of May 1661. It was a quarter to nine in the evening and she was in the midst of prayer when she had a sudden feeling that Father De Brebeuf wanted her to ask God not to let their church be used any more by magicians and evil spirits. After prayer, she settled down to sleep but was interrupted by one of the sisters who came to say that the church doors could not be closed properly because an evil spirit had got into the lock, so would Mother Catherine come and exorcise it? At first Mother Catherine resisted, but then Father De Brebeuf told her she must go and close the door because the evil spirits had decided to hold a Sabbat in the church and steal the consecrated Hosts for magical purposes. So Mother Catherine went down to the church where she found that an evil spirit had indeed lodged itself inside the lock. She blew into the hole, but the spirit struck her hard across the face and left it swollen for the rest of the following day. But then Mother Catherine blew into the lock again and the spirit left, allowing the key to operate properly [**130**, *25–7, 41–53, 94–5*].

Several points about this story are interesting. One wonders, for example, why the priest was unable, or at least thought himself unable, to perform the necessary exorcism, but felt it necessary to send for a nun, albeit a senior and experienced nun, to do it for him. He had, after all, the requisite power as part of his preliminary admission to lesser orders. What is more, it seems he had had some kind of intuition or spirit-message that the convent church was to be desecrated that night, and yet did not think he could prevent its happening. For that, the particular power of Mother Catherine was required. If we forget for a moment that we are dealing with a priest and a nun, the situation could almost be that of a cunning woman and her client who is asking her to use her special powers to unwitch an object. Secondly, one notes how attendance at the Sabbat and stealing the consecrated wafers are activities which have been transferred from human witches to evil spirits. This is most unusual and no explanation is given for it. Thirdly, Mother Catherine's blowing into the lock may look like a simple action intended to remove a physical obstruction, but in this context it can also be, and could have been at the time, interpreted as symbolic, as when Jesus breathed the gift of the Holy Spirit into his disciples (John 20: 22). Mother Catherine, therefore, is presented as a figure of more than natural power. Change the circumstances, and her actions and abilities might almost be interpreted as those of a witch.

Barbe Hallé's original possession was attributed to the malice of a male worker of magic, a servant in the same household, whose declarations of love she had rejected; and a similar motive caused René Besnard magically to inflict impotence on a newly-married couple in 1657 [**130**, *65–78*]. But possession was not the only occult manifestation experienced by the inhabitants of Quebec. We also find examples of *veneficium* (poisonous magic), bewitching by means of a wax image, and various divinatory practices – all importations from the world of European magic – as well as the presence of a werewolf in the province, reported by the *Gazette de Québec* in 1767 and 1776 [**130**, *124–9, 97–101, 113–15, 37–40*].

The phrasing of these last is interesting. In 1767, the report speaks of a werewolf which had been drifting about the neighbourhood for several years. At one point, it had been holed up in its lair but had then burst out and proceeded to inflict serious damage wherever it went. The tone of the piece gives no indication, apart from the use of the term 'loup garoux', that anything more extraordinary than a wild animal was involved. Ten years later, however, the werewolf was characterised by the same journal as a beggar who used to stop people and promise to get them whatever they wanted, although in the very next sentence it describes him as an animal who came to Quebec on his two hind legs, departing the following day with the intention of carrying on as far as Montreal. Clearly the animal was able to convey its future intentions if the journal's informants knew its intended destination, and the journal warned the public to beware of the creature as they would a ravening wolf. The implied simile is significant. Moreover, the editor remarked that the journal had received a further anecdote about him, which was so fantastic that he had refused to publish it. What we may find worth noting, however, in the light of this disclaimer, is the fact that the editor was perfectly happy to record, without any apparent reservation, the news that the creature causing havoc throughout the province was a werewolf.

8

The Decline in Prosecutions

'Scepticism'

Doubts over certain aspects of magic and witchcraft theory surfaced, as we have seen, quite early during the growth of what one might call the classical witchcraft phenomenon in Western Europe. The tenth-century *Canon Episcopi*, for example, had condemned those who subscribed to the belief that certain women rode through the air in the train of the pagan goddess Diana; Alfonso de Spina, confessor to Juan II of Castile (1405–54), wrote that women who admitted their attendance at a Sabbat were merely the victims of diabolically inspired dreams and fantasies, as did the French physician Symphorien Champier (1472–1539) who said, 'they believe that things which exist only within their powerful imagination actually exist beyond the boundaries of their mind', and drew the conclusion that therefore magistrates should beware such women's confessions because 'they confess more things which are mistaken than things which are factually true'.

Protestants, too, expressed doubt on the same range of subjects, and perhaps the most notable of these (certainly the most notorious in their time) were Reginald Scot, an English country gentleman, and Johann Wier or Weyer, a German physician. Both men have in common a strong, not to say a rabid anti-Catholicism, which means that their books should be read with this confessional intent firmly to the fore in the reader's mind. Wier (1515?–88) was a Lutheran, court physician to Duke William V of Cleves-Mark-Jülich-Berg, and had spent four years, from the ages of fourteen to eighteen, as an apprentice in the household of Agrippa von Nettesheim, perhaps the most famous Hermetic magician of the early sixteenth century. Wier was not there to learn magic, of course, but medicine. Nevertheless, he would undoubtedly have had a chance to pick up a certain amount of occult information, as Agrippa's best-known work, *De Occulta Philosophia*, was published during the time of Wier's apprenticeship.

Wier's own work on witchcraft, *De Praestigiis Daemonum* (The Deceptive Tricks of Evil Spirits), was published in 1563 and Wier kept adding material to each subsequent edition until the last in 1583. The scepticism for which he is famous is, in fact, limited. He accepts the reality of the Devil, for example, who, he maintains, has taken over the Catholic Church, using its superstitious rites and ceremonies to further his own cause. Satan sometimes pretends to be a ghost, thereby terrifying simple-minded people, whom he also makes believe that it is necessary for church bells to be baptised and exorcised (Book 1, chapter 11); and Catholic priests are little more than magicians of their Church, who claim to exorcise evil spirits and cure diabolical illnesses, and yet are no more than conscious deceivers of the people (Book 5, chapters 2 and 3).

Witches, on the other hand, are merely senile, simple-minded women peculiarly open to delusion, either self-inflicted or caused by Satan, mentally unstable, prone to melancholia, and sometimes liable to be the object of a false accusation of working malefice. The real villains are those magicians, whom Wier has been describing earlier – priests, monks, poisoners, diviners and cunning folk. These people, he says, falsely boast that they can detect and cure *maleficia*; and if they come across a disease they do not recognise, they accuse some innocent woman of causing it. Those who deserve punishment, therefore, are not the poor, sick, deluded females but the magicians who prey on people's credulity and claim to have occult powers, when they have nothing of the kind (Book 3, chapter 11; Book 6, chapter 1).

In the foreword to his book, Wier protests against what he calls 'the bloodbath of the innocents', an apparent call to end the trials for witchcraft and their subsequent executions; but we must remember that Wier also called for the execution of all those who were allies of the Devil, and it may be this attempt to have the argument both ways which caused his arguments to be rejected by his fellow Lutheran, the Elector of Saxony, in 1572. To the Elector, as indeed to other Protestant princes in Germany, it seemed evident that Catholic perceptions of witchcraft were correct. Witches abounded in spite of the trials and burnings, and this was not the time for anyone to be turning soft [11].

Reginald Scot, on the other hand, was thorough-going in his rejection of virtually all spiritual agency in human affairs, regardless of whether that agency were good or bad. The only form of occult science to which he was prepared to allow a certain legitimacy and effectiveness was natural magic and, in spite of the title of his book – *The Discoverie of Witchcraft* – the main thrust of his argument is directed against magic as a whole, not just that part of it attributed specifically to witches. Scot seems to have been moved to write the *Discoverie*, however, by certain trials for witchcraft, which took place in Essex in 1582 and of which he may have had some personal knowledge, his own book being published in 1584. Now, there was a strain of anti-Catholicism running through that whole episode and, just like Wier, Scot was virulently anti-Catholic, as his discussion of exorcism in Book 15, for example, makes amply clear.

> Surelie this was most common among moonkes and friers, who mainteined their religion, their lust, their liberties, their pompe, their wealth, their estimation and knaverie by such cousening practises. Now I will shew you more speciall orders of popish conjurations, that are so shameleslie admitted into the church of *Rome*, that they are not onelie suffered, but commanded to be used, not by night secretlie, but by daie impudentlie.
>
> (Book 15, chapter 23)

For Scot, investigation of magic involved a reinterpretation of the intellectual authority underlying and supporting the edifice of magical thought. Miracles, wonders, evil spirits, angels, the frequent intervention by supernatural or preternatural agencies in the workings of creation, especially in relation to human affairs – all these he thought needed to be questioned; and since so many of them appeared in the Bible and rested their veracity upon that simple fact, Scot was obliged to venture into the minefield of scriptural scholarship. He devotes large parts of Books 6–13, for example, to discussing (with ample illustration) the exact meaning of various Hebrew words for magical operators and comes to the conclusion that Hebrew philology offers no support for belief in the reality of witches; and when it comes to the well-known story about the witch of Endor who summoned up the ghost of Samuel to answer questions posed by Saul (a simple act of necromancy), Scot dismisses the whole episode as a trick. 'Let us confesse that *Samuell* was not raised . . . and see whether this illusion may not be contrived by the art and cunning of the woman, without anie of these supernaturall devices: for I could cite a hundred papisticall and cousening practises, as difficult as this, and as cleanlie handled' (Book 7, chapter 10). Yet again, Scot's confessional bias and intentions are made manifest, for the context of this last remark is his desire to refute the French Catholic demonologist, Jean Bodin.

But his attacks on Bodin and the other frequently cited writers on occult subjects were only part of a larger preoccupation. Should one rely upon the Bible or upon Catholic accretions and credulity? That is his first question, and his answers make him a straightforward Protestant apologist. His second question, however – how should we interpret the Bible? – takes him beyond confessional polemics and brings him into potentially dangerous theological territory. For by denying the intervention of spirits in human affairs, Scot raises the problem of miracles, not merely whether they happened only in New Testament times and have now disappeared, but whether there is reason to think that while the miracles of the Old Testament may be dubious, those of the New should not be treated to the same degree of scepticism. His answer was a flat proclamation of belief in the veracity of some Scriptural accounts as opposed to others, thus providing himself and his readers with a fudge. His brand of scepticism, then, cannot be said to be that of a modern rationalist, but it was sufficiently unorthodox and sweeping for him to be isolated among contemporary writers on demonology. In effect, however, his aim was not scepticism but reform. For he seems to have been motivated principally by religious considerations, a desire to pare away from the official version of Protestantism in the England of his time what he perceived as superstition (i.e., in his eyes largely Catholic modes of belief and remnant practices), while also distancing himself from the hell-fire Puritanism so influential in his part of the east of England [3; 131, 50–7].

Changes in educated belief

The scepticism of Wier and Scot and their sixteenth-century contemporaries, however, turns out to have consisted either of doubts, based upon intellectual or theological arguments, about the claims made by various people, including witches themselves, to be able to produce preternatural effects; or of doubts based on polemical intentions in what was essentially a series of confessional wars, with academic disagreement as their method of fighting. Nevertheless, Scot's preoccupation with the correct way to interpret scripture and find a sure, authoritative basis for belief was taken up in the later seventeenth century. One can see it in the work of Balthasar Bekker (1634–98), for example, a Dutch Protestant minister who published a monumental four-part work on magic and witchcraft, *De Betoverde Weereld* (The World Bewitched) in 1692–3, arguing against the temporal activity of the Devil and evil spirits, and against the reality of all kinds of magical operation and manifestation, including witchcraft and demonic possession. Bekker makes two principal points: (1) it is superstition which causes people to believe in witchcraft and sustains the existence of cunning folk and 'unwitchers' (i.e., those who specialise in lifting magic laid on by others); and (2) many, if not most, opinions on demonology are based on mistaken biblical exegesis. Needless to say, this second development brought him into conflict with the Dutch Reformed Church, and it is actually this aspect of magic and the belief in spirits which informs *The World Bewitched* and makes Bekker less a champion of Enlightenment rationalism and more a religious controversialist, ready to employ Cartesian philosophical arguments against the temporal activity of evil spirits in an internal, ecclesiastical debate [134].

Still, the fact that the book was quickly translated into French, German and English meant that its ideas could be picked up and absorbed by a wider audience. His Cartesianism, indeed, is an important factor in his argument, for Descartes's sceptical methodology, and conviction that the universe was an orderly machine which functioned according to fixed laws and had no need of or place for any interference by God or spirits, meant that the whole basis of demonology upon which magic rested was called into question. The particularly Protestant emphasis on the omnipotence of God had had its effect over the years, too. It was a divine attribute which the period of intense prosecution of witches had tended to obscure, allowing Satan to loom perhaps over-large in the workings of creation. But with God restored, as it were, to his necessary supremacy, Satan and his attendant evil spirits were diminished and their agency called into serious question. Then, with God himself removed from immediate interest in or responsibility for human affairs in particular and the running of the universe in general, the rational ground for the existence of demonological theory more or less vanished. Stuart Clark sums up the new situation as follows: 'When natural theology was replaced by rational theology – and theism by deism – it became unnecessary to impose causal activity on passive matter or find spiritual testimony to illustrate this' [31, 299].

Bekker was by no means the only figure to find fault with demonology and its related ideas, of course. A professor of law at the newly founded University of Halle, Christian Thomasius (1655–1728) came to disbelieve in a personal Devil, denied the existence of the diabolic pact and praised Descartes for dispersing those scholastic fantasies, as he called them, which had kept belief in witchcraft and evil spirits alive for so long; while in France, Voltaire defined magic as 'the secret of doing what nature cannot do', and dismissed it as an impossibility, as did other French *philosophes* and *encyclopédistes* who railed against 'superstition' in all its guises. 'Reason' became the supreme arbiter to which the new generation of philosophers appealed, reason being, in the words of an English Dissenting minister, John Toland, 'the only foundation of all certitude, and . . . nothing revealed, whether as to its nature or existence, is more exempted from its disquisitions than the ordinary phenomena of nature' (*Christianity Not Mysterious*, 1696).

It was an intellectual stance which affected more than religion, of course. Medicine, too, increasingly relied on natural explanations for disease and illnesses and less upon those involving divine anger, punishment for sin, or intervention by spirits [110, 219–35], and both Catholic and Protestant states began to put aside their previous enthusiasm for creating the ideal, godly community, a political change which rendered it less likely that Church or state would continue to support popular demands for widespread prosecution of dissidents such as witches [79, 33–44].

Nevertheless, we should not run away with the idea that changes in educated belief were uniform all over Europe and at any given time; nor should we assume that these changes were sufficient by themselves to bring to an end the process of witchcraft prosecution. First, as Wilkins reminds us, 'although belief in the demonic origin of witchcraft and possession was progressively nullified in the eighteenth century, it is interesting to note that the subject retained a degree of popularity with the educated public' [145, 307], an observation she directs at France but which is true of Europe as a whole. Secondly, the pressure for prosecution did not often come from above: rather it stemmed from below as neighbour accused neighbour and insisted, as far as possible, in bringing the accused to court. The decline of prosecutions, therefore, should not be seen as evidence that belief in magic and witchcraft was disappearing completely from eighteenth-century society, polite or rustic. On the contrary, there are plenty of indications that it remained strong in those sections of society where it always had been strong.

This can be illustrated by one of Joseph Addison's essays in *The Spectator*, published on Saturday, 14 July 1711. His favourite character, Sir Roger de Coverley, he says, and he were walking beside a wood when an old woman applied to them for charity.

[Sir Roger] told me that this very old Woman had the Reputation of a Witch all over the Country, that her Lips were observed to be always in motion, and that there was not a Switch about her House which her Neighbours did not believe had carried her several hundreds of Miles.... There was not a Maid in the Parish that would take a Pin from her, though she should offer a Bag of Money with it.... Sir Roger, who is a little puzzled about the old Woman, [advised] her as a Justice of Peace to avoid all Communication with the Devil, and never to hurt any of her Neighbours' Cattle.... On our Return home, Sir Roger told me that old *Moll* had been often brought before him for making Children spit Pins, and giving Maids the Night-Mare; and that the Country People would be tossing her into a Pond and trying Experiments with her every Day, if it was not for him and his Chaplain. I have since found, upon Enquiry, that Sir Roger was several times staggered with the Reports that had been brought him concerning this old Woman, and would frequently have bound her over to the County Sessions, had not his Chaplain with much ado perswaded him to the contrary.

The representative of the Church, then, may have had his doubts about the old woman's status as a witch, but the magistrate, despite hesitations, apparently did not and neither had the country folk among whom both they and the old woman lived. Defence of the belief of this majority would have been straightforward a hundred, or even fifty years earlier. Now, however, the intellectual grounds for its defence had shifted, and in consequence those who still undertook to ward off theological and philosophical criticisms found that the old arguments were less likely to be taken with any degree of seriousness by modern men of learning.

Changes in judicial procedure

More significant and perhaps more important than changes in philosophical discourse, however, were changes in judicial procedure. Again, these did not appear suddenly. As early as 1640, for example, the Parlement of Paris had arranged that it should receive an automatic appeal from anyone convicted of witchcraft in any other French court – nothing to do with intellectual scepticism on the part of the Parisian judges: rather, they were concerned with high standards of justice and wished to make sure these were maintained in provincial courts outwith their immediate control [**132**, *I* & *II*]. This kind of legal unease in the face of judicial incompetence or disregard for legality was fuelled by a number of books in which the author, without necessarily surrendering his acceptance of the basic realities of the magical or spirit-invested universe, criticised the way in which the legal system operated in cases of witchcraft, especially in courts removed from centres of government. In 1631, for example, the Jesuit Friedrich von Spee published his *Cautio Criminalis* (Taking Precautions in Criminal Cases), a treatise which summarised in vivid detail the excesses and illegalities of contemporary judicial investigation of witches, and condemned them outright; and he was followed by the Lutheran Professor of Theology at the University of Erfurt, Johann Meyfart, whose *Christliche Erinnerung* (Christian Memory), published in 1636, covered more or less the same ground and came to the same kind of conclusions.

Now, these things could be interconnected. Spee's book was translated into French in 1660; attempts by the provinces of Normandy, Guyenne and Bearn in the 1670s to resist the authority claimed by Paris were quashed by the Crown's chief minister, Jean Colbert; and between 1678 and 1681 the French Court was rocked by a scandal (*l'Affaire des poisons*), involving the King's mistress, a notorious poisoner and worker of harmful magic, and a series of blasphemous pseudo-religious ceremonies reminiscent of what would later be called 'Black Masses'. These were some of the steps which led to the King's issuing an edict in 1682 which reclassified witchcraft as a superstition and removed the death penalty from witchcraft cases except where these involved sacrilege and poisoning [**79**, *48–53*], and this combination of well-documented criticism of judicial illegalities, particularly in provincial courts, and the politicisation of witchcraft beliefs, allied to growing scepticism among some in the educated classes, provides a paradigm for decline of prosecution in European countries other than France [22, 108–38; 43, 176–7]. One obvious exception, however, is Hungary where decline in the number of witch-prosecutions was linked to a rise of fear of vampires, and it was actually notice of a particular vampire case in 1755 which alerted Empress Maria Theresa to what two of her court physicians called 'superstition', and caused her to issue edicts in 1755 and 1756 ordering the prohibition of activities which had their roots in traditional occult beliefs, and the transference of all current witch-trials to her own courts of appeal [69, 168–88].

Changes in judicial attitudes and procedure may be summarised as follows: (a) local officials, who were overwhelmingly the principal official movers in witch-trials, were brought under centralised control; (b) in Germany, the law faculties of the universities promoted judicial caution in crimes of witchcraft (in those countries where the Inquisition operated, such caution and care for legality had long been officially required); (c) the use of torture in witchcraft investigations was restricted and then prohibited. George Mackenzie, Lord Advocate of Scotland from 1677 to 1686, criticised those inferior judges whom he considered to be incompetent in trials for witchcraft, and condemned their use of torture to extract confessions – an interesting example of someone who was jealous of the reputation of the law even though he himself was not a sceptic when it came to belief in the reality of witches; (d) courts began to require a higher standard of evidence from witnesses, placing a heavier burden of responsibility upon the prosecution to prove its case rather than rely upon confessions from the accused; (e) defence advocates, long a standard feature of Scottish criminal trials, began to appear in witchcraft trials elsewhere; and (f) the cost of prosecutions, always heavy, gradually became more than the suspect witch's community was prepared to bear [79, 7–33]

Concluding Remarks

Recent research has modified quite a number of previous assumptions or generalisations about witches and witchcraft. It has become clear, for example, that the equation of persecution of witches with persecution of women is over-simple, since witches were by no means exclusively female and they were taken to court not on a charge of being women but of being witches. Their crime, in other words, was not gender-specific [75, 79–91]. Witchcraft, indeed, and the whole related range of magical activities attributed to those individuals put on trial for them tended to affect those spheres of human life particularly associated with women – childbirth, preparation of food, care for animals, tending the sick – and the resentments which eventually called forth acts of malefice were frequently embodied in that special female form, the exchange of injurious words [111, 91–118]. Not surprisingly, therefore, women featured large in the number of those accused of these types of magic.

Nor did an accusation of and trial for witchcraft automatically result in a verdict of guilty and sentence of execution. Many were accused, but far fewer brought to trial, and of those who were tried even fewer were executed. The death toll must, of course, include those unfortunates who committed suicide or died of neglect or violence or disease while in prison awaiting trial. But even so, and bearing in mind that full investigation of surviving European archives has only just begun, the number of those who were put to death as witches during the early modern period is small. One should bear in mind, perhaps, by way of comparison, the number of people who were executed on other criminal charges. The majority of these were men, yet no one speaks of a deliberate persecution of men or seeks to blame the patriarchal structure of society for putting them to death.

Nor did witchcraft trials occur uniformly all over Europe at any given historical period. They flourished from time to time in states or regions especially where the control of central government was uncertain, thereby allowing local magistrates or clergy a relatively free hand to bow to any popular demand for prosecution. In larger, more centralised states, the government tended to exercise firmer control over the administration of justice and this often either prevented an outburst of witch- prosecution altogether, or kept it within bounds. The Church, whether Catholic or Protestant, did not play a prominent role in these trials except in those German states where the ecclesiastic was also the territorial ruler, or perhaps in Scotland where the Kirk was particularly anxious to establish its own theocratic society.

Outbursts did not last long, perhaps two or three years at most, before a period of calm was restored; and when one reads of 'large hunts', it is worth remembering that these were rarely unified affairs directed by a single, purposeful authority or individual, but rather a conglomeration of small incidents made to look big because they occurred within a relatively short space of time and the accused were often fetched to a major administrative centre to be tried at a distance from their local community where the offences had taken place. Moreover, to reiterate a point made earlier in this book, witches were accused of and tried for activities declared criminal and forbidden by national statute. Lynching was rare. The process by which the defendants' guilt or innocence was established was a judicial one, however flawed the administration of its procedures may often have been, and such emotive terms as 'hunt' or 'craze' or 'mania' to describe these episodes are therefore inappropriate and, indeed, wide of the mark [78, *156–61*].

Finally, one should observe that belief in magic and witchcraft did not die out in eighteenth-century Europe, even among the educated classes. These, to be sure, took an official line and proclaimed that magic and witchcraft were mere superstition; but this had been said by many Catholic and Protestant scholars long before the 'enlightenment', and their dismissal by the learned of later centuries smacks somewhat of self-congratulation on the one hand and social snobbery on the other, since it became an almost universal assumption among them that magic and witchcraft were now to be found only in peasant (i.e. unlearned) communities – a false and biased belief, as any study of the survival of magic and witchcraft in the nineteenth and twentieth centuries will soon bear out.

Bibliography

[1] B. Andenmatten and K. U. Tremp: 'De l'hérésie à la sorcellerie: l'inquisiteur Ulric de Torrenté OP (vers 1420–1445) et l'affermisse-ment de l'inquisition en suisse romande', Zeitschrift für schweizerische Kirchengeschichte, 86 (1992), pp. 69–119.

[2] S. Anglo (ed.): The Damn'd Art (London 1977).

[3] ——: 'Reginald Scot's Discoverie of Witchcraft: Scepticism and Sad-duceeism', in Anglo (ed.): The Damn'd Art (1977), pp. 106–39.

[4] B. Ankarloo: 'Magies scandinaves et sorciers du Nord'. in Muchembled (ed.): Magie et sorcellerie en Europe (1994), pp. 195–213.

[5] B. Ankarloo and G. Henningsen (eds): Early Modern European Witch-craft (Clarendon, Press, 1990).

[6] G. Audisio: The Waldensian Dissent: Persecution and Survival, c.1170–c.1570 (Cambridge University Press, 1999).

[7] J. Axtell: The Invasion Within: The Contest of Cultures in Colonial North America (Oxford University Press, 1985).

[8] M. Bailey: 'The Mediaeval Concept of the Witches' Sabbath', Exem-plaria, 8 (1996), pp. 419–39.

[9] J. Barry, M. Hester and G. Roberts (eds): Witchcraft in Early Modern Europe (Clarendon Press, 1990).

[10] R. Bartlett: Trial by Fire and Water: The Mediaeval Judicial Ordeal (Clar-endon Press, 1986).

[11] C. Baxter: 'Johann Weyer's De Praestigiis Daemonum: Unsystematic Psychopathology', in Anglo (ed.): The Damn'd Art (1977), pp. 53–75.

[12] G. Bechtel: Le sorcier et l'Occident (Paris: Plon, 1997).

[13] W. Behringer: 'Kinderhexenprozesse: zur Rolle von Kindern in der Geschichte der Hexenverfolgung', Zeitschrift für historische Forschung, 16 (1989), pp. 31–47.

[14] ——: 'Weather, Hunger, and Fear: Origins of the European Witch-hunts in Climate, Society, and Mentality', German History, 13 (1995), pp. 1–27.

[15] ——: Witchcraft Persecutions in Bavaria (Cambridge University Press, 1997).

[16] F. Bethencourt: 'Portugal: a Scrupulous Inquisition', in Ankarloo and Henningsen (eds): Early Modern European Witchcraft (1990), pp. 403–22.

[17] L. Binz: 'Les débuts de la chasse aux sorcières dans la diocèse de Genève', Bibliothèque d'Humanisme et Renaissance, 59 (1997), pp. 561–81.

[18] A. Blamires (ed.): Woman Defamed and Woman Defended (Clarendon Press, 1992).

[19] W. Blécourt, de: 'Cunning Women, from Healers to Fortune Tellers', in H. Binnefeld and R. Dekker (eds): Curing and Insuring (Hilversum Verloren, 1993), pp. 43–55.

111

[20]   E. H. Boone: *Incarnations of the Aztec Supernatural*, Transactions of the American Philosophical Society, **79**, part 2 (1989), pp. 55–83.

[21]   A. Borst: *Mediaeval Worlds: Barbarians, Heretics, and Artists in the Middle Ages* (University of Chicago, 1992).

[22]   I. Bostridge: *Witchcraft and its Transformations, c.1650–c.1750* (Clarendon Press, 1997).

[23]   S. Brauner: *Fearless Wives and Frightened Shrews* (University of Massachusetts Press, 1995).

[24]   R. Briggs: 'Many Reasons Why: Witchcraft and the Problem of Multiple Explanation', in Barry, Hester and Roberts (eds): *Witchcraft in Early Modern Europe* (1990), pp. 49–63.

[25]   J. A. Brundage: *Mediaeval Canon Law* (Longman, 1995).

[26]   J. Casey: *Early Modern Spain* (Routledge, 1999).

[27]   C. Cassar: *Witchcraft, Sorcery, and the Inquisition: A Study of Cultural Values in Early Modern Malta* (Malta: Mireva, 1996).

[28]   F. Cervantes: *The Devil in the New World: The Impact of Diabolism in New Spain* (Yale University Press, 1994).

[29]   S. Clark: 'King James's Daemonologie: Witchcraft and Kingship', in Anglo (ed.): *The Damn'd Art* (1977), pp. 156–81.

[30]   ——: 'Protestant Demonology: Sin, Superstition, and Society, c.1520–c.1630', in Ankarloo and Hemmingsen (eds): *Early Modern European Witchcraft* (1990), pp. 45–81.

[31]   ——: *Thinking with Demons* (Oxford University Press, 1998).

[32]   S. Colin: 'The Wild Man and the Indian in Early 16th Century Book Illustration', in C. F. Feest (ed.): *Indians and Europe* (Alano, Aachen, 1989), pp. 5–36.

[33]   J. Cooke: 'Nice Young Girls and Wicked Old Witches: the "Rightful Age" of Women in Middle English Verse', in E. Mullally and J. Thompson (eds): *The Court and Cultural Diversity* (Boydell and Brewer, 1997), pp. 219–28.

[34]   D. Cressy: *Coming Over: Migration and Communication between England and New England in the Seventeenth Century* (Cambridge University Press, 1987).

[35]   L. Daston and K. Park: *Wonders and the Order of Nature, 1150–1750* (Zone Books, 1998).

[36]   J. P. Davidson : 'Great Black Goats and Evil Little Women: the Image of the Witch in Sixteenth-Century German Art', *Journal of the Rocky Mountain Mediaeval and Renaissance Association*, **6** (1985), pp. 141–57.

[37]   J. P. Demos: *Entertaining Satan: Witchcraft and the Culture of Early New England* (Oxford University Press, 1982).

[38]   T. Dömötör, 'The Cunning Folk in English and Hungarian Witch Trials', in V. J. Newall (ed.): *Folklore Studies in the Twentieth Century* (Rowman and Littlefield, 1980), pp. 183–87.

[39]   L. Dresen-Coenders (ed.): *Saints and She-Devils: Images of Women in the Fifteenth and Sixteenth Centuries* (Rubicon, 1987).

[40]   E. Duffy: *The Stripping of the Altars* (Yale University Press, 1992).

[41]   A. Dundes (ed.): *The Evil Eye: A Folklore Casebook* (Garland Publishing, 1981).

[42] R. C. Ellison: 'The Kirkjuból Affair: a Seventeenth-Century Icelandic Witchcraft Case Analysed', *The Seventeenth Century*, 8 (1993), pp. 217–43.

[43] P. Elmer: 'Saints or Sorcerers: Quakerism, Demonology, and the Decline of Witchcraft in Seventeenth-Century England', in Barry, Hester and Roberts (eds): *Witchcraft in Early Modern Europe* (1990), pp. 145–79.

[44] R. J. Evans: *Rituals of Retribution* (Penguin, 1996).

[45] E. E. Evans-Pritchard: *Witchcraft, Oracles and Magic among the Azande* (Oxford University Press, 1937).

[46] R. C. Finucane: *Miracles and Pilgrims* (Macmillan, 1977).

[47] R. Fletcher: *The Conversion of Europe, from Paganism to Christianity, 371–1386 A D* (Harper Collins, 1997).

[48] A. Foa: 'The Witch and the Jew, Two Alikes that were not the Same', in J. Cohen (ed.): *From Witness to Witchcraft* (Harrassowitz Verlag, 1996), pp. 361–74.

[49] M. Gaskill: 'The Devil in the Shape of a Man Witchcraft, Conflict and Belief in Jacobean England', *Historical Research* 71 (1998), pp. 142–71.

[50] R. Godbeer: *The Devil's Dominion: Magic and Religion in Early New England* (Cambridge University Press, 1993).

[51] A. Golding (trans.): *The Sermons of John Calvin* (London, 1583).

[52] F. Graf: *Magic in the Ancient World* (Harvard University Press, 1997).

[53] S. Grundy: 'The Viking's Mother: Relations between Mothers and their Grown Sons in Icelandic Sagas', in J. C. Parsons and B. Wheeler (eds): *Mediaeval Mothering* (Garland, 1996), pp. 223–37.

[54] S. Gruzinski: *The Conquest of Mexico* (Polity Press, 1993).

[55] D. D. Hall (ed.): *Witch-Hunting in Seventeenth-Century New England* (Northeastern University Press, 1991).

[56] K. Harstrup: *Nature and Policy in Iceland, 1400–1800* (Oxford University Press, 1990).

[57] ——: 'Iceland: Sorcerers and Paganism', in Ankarloo and Henningsen (eds): *Early Modern European Witchcraft* (1990), pp. 383–401.

[58] G. Henningsen: *The Witches' Advocate: Basque Witchcraft and the Spanish Inquisition, 1609–1614* (University of Nevada, 1980).

[59] L. C. Hults: 'Baldung and the Witches of Freiburg: the Evidence of Images', *Journal of Interdisciplinary History*, 18 (1987), pp. 249–76.

[60] N. Jacques-Chaquin and M. Préaud (eds): *Le sabbat des sorciers, XVe–XVIIIe siècles* (Jérôme Millon, 1993).

[61] ——: *Les sorciers du carroi de Marlou: un procès de sorcellerie en Berry, 1582–3* (Jérôme Millon, 1996).

[62] P. F. Jensen: 'Calvin and Witchcraft', *Reformed Theological Review*, 34 (1975), pp. 76–86.

[63] J. C. V. Johansen: 'Denmark: the Sociology of Accusations', in Ankarloo and Henningsen (eds): *Early Modern European Witchcraft* (1990), pp. 339–65.

[64] S. I. Johnston: 'Defining the Dreadful: Remarks on the Greek Child-killing Demon', in M. Meyer and P. Mirecki (eds): *Ancient Magic and Ritual Power* (E. J. Brill, 1995), pp. 361–87.

[65]   C. F. Karlsen: *The Devil in the Shape of a Woman: Witchcraft in Colonial New England* (Norton, 1998).

[66]   R. Kieckhefer: *European Witch Trials* (Routledge and Kegan Paul, 1976).

[67]   ——: *Magic in the Middle Ages* (Cambridge University Press, 1989).

[68]   G. Klaniczay : 'Hungary: the Accusations and the Universe of Popular Magic', in Ankarloo and Henningsen (eds): *Early Modern European Witchcraft* (1990), pp. 219–55.

[69]   ——: *The Uses of Supernatural Power* (Polity Press, 1990).

[70]   ——: 'Le sabbat raconté par les témoins des procès de sorcellerie en Hongrie', in Jacques-Chaquin and Préaud (eds): *Le Sabbat des Sorciers* (1993), pp. 227–46.

[71]   ——: 'Bûchers tardifs en Europe centrale et orientale', in Muchembled (ed.): *Magie et Sorcellerie en Europe* (1994), pp. 215–31.

[72]   J. H. Langbein: *Prosecuting Crime in the Renaissance* (Harvard University Press, 1974).

[73]   C. Larner: *Enemies of God: The Witch-Hunt in Scotland* (Blackwell, 1983).

[74]   ——: 'Crimen Exceptum: the Crime of Witchcraft in Europe', in her *Witchcraft and Religion: The Politics of Popular Belief* (Blackwell, 1984), pp. 35–67.

[75]   ——: 'Witchcraft Past and Present', in her *Witchcraft and Religion* (1984), pp. 79–91.

[76]   A. C. Lehmann and J. E. Myer (eds): *Magic, Witchcraft and Religion*, 2nd edn (Mayfield, 1989).

[77]   H. Lehmann: 'The Persecution of Witches as Restoration of Order: the Case of Germany, 1590s–1650s', *Central European History*, **21** (1988), pp. 107–21.

[78]   B. P. Levack: *The Witch-Hunt in Early Modern Europe* (Longman, 1987).

[79]   ——: 'The Decline and End of Witchcraft Prosecutions', in B. Ankarloo and S. Clark (eds): *The Athlone History of Witchcraft and Magic in Europe*, vol. 5 (Athlone Press, 1999), pp. 3–93.

[80]   G. Lizerand: *Le dossier de l'affaire des Templiers* (Les Belles Lettres, 1964).

[81]   S. MacCormack: 'Demons, Imagination, and the Incas', in S. Greenblatt (ed.): *New World Encounters* (University of California, 1993), pp. 101–26.

[82]   ——: 'Limits of Understanding: Perceptions of Greco-Roman and Amerindian Paganism in Early Modern Europe', in K. O. Kupperman (ed.): *America in European Consciousness, 1493–1750* (University of North Carolina Press, 1995), pp. 79–129.

[83]   B. McGinn: *Anti-Christ* (HarperCollins, 1996).

[84]   J. T. McNeill and H. M. Gamer: *Mediaeval Handbooks of Penance* (Columbia University Press, 1938).

[85]   E. Maier: *Trente ans avec le diable, une nouvelle chasse aux sorciers sur la Riviera lémanique, 1477–1484* (Lausanne, 1996).

[86]   P. G. Maxwell-Stuart: 'The Fear of the King is Death', in W. G. Naphy and P. Roberts (eds): *Fear in Early Modern Europe* (Manchester University Press, 1997), pp. 209–25.

[87]   ——: 'Witchcraft in Aberdeenshire, 1597–8', *Northern Scotland*, **18** (1998), pp. 1–14.

[88]   ——: *The Occult in Early Modern Europe: A Documentary History* (Macmillan, 1999).

[89]   J. Middleton and E. H. Winter: *Witchcraft and Sorcery in East Africa* (Routledge & Kegan Paul, 1963).

[90]   L. J. R. Milis (ed.): *The Pagan Middle Ages* (Boydell Press, 1998).

[91]   S. A. Mitchell: 'Nordic Witchcraft in Transition', *Scandia*, **63** (1997), pp. 17–33.

[92]   E. W. Monter: 'Witchcraft in Geneva, 1537–1662', *Journal of Modern History*, **43** (1971), pp. 179–204.

[93]   ——: 'Les enfants du sabbat: bilan provisoire', in Jacques-Chaquin and Préaud (eds): *Le sabbat des sorciers* (1993), pp. 383–8.

[94]   ——: 'Scandinavian Witchcraft in Anglo-American Perspective', in Ankarloo and Henningsen (eds): *Early Modern European Witchcraft* (1990), pp. 425–34.

[95]   ——: 'Toads and Eucharists: the Male Witches of Normandy, 1564–1660', *French Historical Studies*, **20** (1997), pp. 563–95.

[96]   F. Mormando: *The Preacher's Demons: Bernardino of Siena and the Social Underworld of Early Renaissance Italy* (University of Chicago Press, 1999).

[97]   K. Morris: *Sorceress or Witch? The Image of Gender in Mediaeval Iceland and Northern Europe* (University Press of America, 1991).

[98]   R. Moss: 'Missionaries and Magicians: the Jesuit Encounter with Native American Shamans on New England's Colonial Frontier', in P. Benes (ed.): *Wonders of the Invisible World, 1600–1900* (Boston University Press, 1995), pp. 17–33.

[99]   R. Muchembled (ed.): *Magie et Sorcellerie en Europe du Moyen Age à nos jours* (Armand Colin, 1994).

[100]   H. E. Naess: 'Norway: the Criminological Context', in Ankarloo and Henningsen (eds): *Early Modern European Witchcraft* (1990), pp. 367–82.

[101]   D. Ogier: 'Night Revels and Werewolfery in Calvinist Guernsey', *Folklore*, **109** (1998), pp. 53–62.

[102]   M. O'Neill: 'Magical Healing, Love Magic, and the Inquisition in Late Sixteenth-Century Modena', in S. Haliczer (ed.): *Inquisition and Society in Early Modern Europe* (Croom Helm, 1987), pp. 88–114.

[103]   M. Ostorero: '*Folâtrer avec les démons': sabbat et chasse aux sorciers à Vevey, 1448* (Lausanne, 1995).

[104]   P. Paravy: 'A propos de la genèse médiévale des chasses aux sorcières: le traité de Claude Tholosan, juge dauphinois (vers 1486)', *Mélanges de l'Ecole Française de Rome*, **91** (1979), pp. 333–79.

[105]   K. Park: 'Medicine and Magic: the Healing Arts', in J. C. Brown and R. C. Davis (eds): *Gender and Society in Renaissance Italy* (Longman, 1998), pp. 129–49.

[106]   G. K. Paster: *The Body Embarrassed* (Cornell University Press, 1993).

[107]   J. L. Pearl: *The Crime of Crimes: Demonology and Politics in France, 1560–1620* (Wilfred Laurier University Press, 1999).

[108] E. Peters: *The Magician, the Witch, and the Law* (University of Pennsylvania, 1978).

[109] E. Pócs: *Between the Living and the Dead* (Central European University Press, 1999).

[110] R. Porter: 'Witches and Magic in Enlightenment, Romantic, and Liberal Thought', in B. Ankarloo and S. Clark (eds): *The Athlone History of Witchcraft and Magic in Europe*, vol. 5 (Athlone Press, 1999), pp. 193–282.

[111] D. Purkiss: *The Witch in History: Early Modern and Twentieth-Century Representations* (Routledge, 1996).

[112] N. Quezada: 'The Inquisition's Repression of Curanderos', in M. E. Perry and A. J. Cruz (eds): *Cultural Encounters: The Impact of the Inquisition in Spain and the New World* (University of California, 1991), pp. 37–57.

[113] J. Rabasa: *Inventing America: Spanish Historiography and the Formation of Eurocentrism* (University of Oklahoma Press, 1993).

[114] R. Rapley: *A Case of Witchcraft: The Trial of Urbain Grandier* (Manchester University Press, 1998).

[115] R. H. Robbins: *The Encyclopaedia of Witchcraft and Demonology* (London, 1959).

[116] G. Romeo: *Inquisitori, esorcisti e streghe nell' Italia della Controriforma* (Florence, Sansoni, 1990).

[117] U. Rublack: *The Crimes of Women in Early Modern Germany* (Clarendon Press, 1999).

[118] G. Ruggiero: *Binding Passions* (Oxford University Press, 1993).

[119] W. Rummel: *Bauern, Herren und Hexen: Studien zur Sozialgeschichte sponheimischer und kurttrierischer Hexenprozesse, 1574–1664* (Göttingen, 1991).

[120] J. B. Russell: *A History of Witchcraft* (Thames Hudson, 1980).

[121] W. F. Ryan: *The Bathhouse at Midnight: Magic in Russia* (Sutton, 1999).

[122] D. W. Sabean: *Power in the Blood* (Cambridge University Press, 1984).

[123] N. Salisbury: *Manitou and Providence: Indians, Europeans, and the Making of New England, 1500–1643* (Oxford University Press, 1982).

[124] F. Salmon and M. Cabré: 'Fascinating Women: the Evil Eye in Medical Scholasticism', in R. French, J. Arrizabalaga, A. Cunningham and L. Garcia-Ballester (eds): *Medicine from the Black Death to the French Disease* (Ashgate, 1998).

[125] G. Scarre: *Witchcraft and Magic in Sixteenth- and Seventeenth-Century Europe* (Macmillan, 1987).

[126] C. Scott Dixon: 'Popular Beliefs and the Reformation in Brandenburg-Ansbach', in Scribner and Johnson (eds): *Popular Religion in Germany and Central Europe, 1400–1800* (1996), pp. 119–39.

[127] R. Scribner and T. Johnson (eds): *Popular Religion in Germany and Central Europe, 1400–1800* (Macmillan, 1996).

[128] H. Sebald: *Witch-Children* (Prometheus Books, 1995).

[129] P. Segl (ed.): *Der Hexenhammer: Entstehung und Umfeld des Malleus Maleficarum* (Böhlau, 1988).

[130] R.-L. Séguin: *La sorcellerie au Québec du xviie au XIXᵉ siècle* (Luméac/Payot, 1978).

[131] J. Sharpe: *Instruments of Darkness: Witchcraft in England, 1550–1750* (Hamish Hamilton, 1996).

[132] A. Soman: *Sorcellerie et justice criminelle (16ᵉ–18ᵉ siècles)* (London, 1992).

[133] P. Sörlin: *Wicked Arts: Witchcraft and Magic Trials in Southern Sweden, 1635–1754* (Brill, 1999).

[134] G. J. Stronks: 'The Significance of Balthasar Bekker's "The Enchanted World"', in M. Gijswijt-Hofstra and W. Frijhoff (eds): *Witchcraft and the Netherlands* (Rotterdam, 1991), pp. 149–56.

[135] J. Tazbir: 'Hexenprozesse in Polen', *Archiv für Reformationsgeschichte*, 71 (1980), pp. 280–307.

[136] J. Tedeschi: *The Prosecution of Heresy* (Binghamton, 1991).

[137] ——: 'Inquisitorial Law and the Witch', in Ankarloo and Henningsen (eds): *Early Modern European Witchcraft* (1990), pp. 83–118.

[138] B. G. Trigger: *Natives and Newcomers: Canada's 'Heroic Age' Reconsidered* (Manchester University Press, 1985).

[139] R.-L. Wagner: *Sorcier et Magicien* (Librairie Droz, 1939).

[140] G. K. Waite: 'Between the Devil and the Inquisitor: Anabaptists, Diabolical Conspiracies, and Magical Beliefs in the Sixteenth Century Netherlands', in W. O. Packull and G. L. Dipple (eds): *Radical Reformation Studies* (Ashgate, 1999), pp. 120–40.

[141] R. Walinski-Kiehl: ' "Godly states": Confessional Conflict and Witch-hunting in Early Modern Germany', *Mentalities*, 5 (1988), pp. 13–24.

[142] ——: 'The Devil's Children: Child Witch-trials in Early Modern Germany', *Continuity and Change*, 11 (1996), pp. 171–89.

[143] D. P. Walker: 'Demonic Possession Used as Propaganda in the Later Sixteenth Century', in P. Rossi (ed.): *Scienze, credenze occulte, livelli di cultura* (Florence, 1982), pp. 237–48.

[144] M. J. Westerkamp: *Women and Religion in Early America, 1600–1850* (Routledge, 1999).

[145] K. S. Wilkins: 'Attitudes to Witchcraft and Demonic Possession in France During the Eighteenth Century', *Journal of European Studies*, 3 (1973), pp. 348–62.

[146] L. H. Willumsen: 'Witches of the High North: the Finnmark Witchcraft Trial in the Seventeenth Century', *Scandinavian Journal of History*, 22 (1997), pp. 199–221.

[147] E. Wilson: 'Institoris in Innsbruck', in R. Scribner and T. Johnson (eds): *Popular Religion in Germany and Central Europe, 1400–1800* (Macmillan, 1996), pp. 87–100.

[148] R. M. Wright: *Art and Antichrist in Mediaeval Europe* (Manchester University Press, 1995).

[149] R. Zguta: 'Witchcraft Trials in Seventeenth-Century Russia', *American Historical Review*, 82 (1977), pp. 1187–207.

[150] ——: 'Witchcraft and Medicine in Pre-Petrine Russia', *The Russian Review*, 37 (1978), pp. 438–48.

Index

118